Private Pilot Test Prep 2023-2024

Theory, Tests, Explanations, Vocabulary & Q&A.
Pass the Exam and Become a Safe Pilot! Include
Audiobook to Learn When & Where You Want.

Edric Howell

Tabla de contenido

INTRODUCTION

The Private Pilot License is a certificate issued by the FAA that allows an individual to fly an aircraft outside of controlled airspace. The Private Pilot License FAA Knowledge Checkride Exams are two tests that require the applicant to demonstrate their knowledge of Private Pilot Flight Manuals. The exam is meant for people who have been holding a Private Pilot Certificate for an aggregate of at least four years and have less than 1500 hours total flight time, including 100 hours as pilot in command. This includes students enrolled in a Single Engine Land rating course or an Instrument Rating course. If you're looking to score well on your knowledge checkride, this will give you all the information you need to succeed!

To begin with, the pass mark is 70%. You must score 70% or higher questions correctly in order to pass. This is true for both the instrument and non-instrument Knowledge Checkride.

The Private Pilot Knowledge Check Ride is a two part test. The first test has 50 questions and the second test has 40. The FAA allows you to miss the first 20% of questions before they consider your knowledge unsatisfactory.

You have 4 hours to take the 50 question Knowledge Checkride; 3 hours and 30 minutes for the 40 question Knowledge Checkride. If your check ride starts at 10 am, you're up against it! You must plan accordingly and maximize your time to study for this exam.

There are two private pilot knowledge tests that cover different areas of flight: Airplane General and Airplane Flight maneuvers. There are also Geographical questions; and information on Private Pilot Flight Manuals. The exam is made up of five domains: Aeronautical Knowledge, Behaviors/Procedures, Airplane General and Instrument Procedures. Then after that there are two more domains; Technical (T) , Rating Information for Aircraft Inspectors (RI), and Aircraft Limitations.

For those who might be first-time pilots, or for those who have taken their license before and are looking to upgrade, the FAA Knowledge Exam is a rigorous test that is designed to assess a pilot's knowledge of the Federal Aviation Regulations. The Knowledge Exam is administered by private pilot examiners at more than 73 locations nationwide.

The knowledge exam includes questions that cover aeronautics and general aviation safety rules and regulations such as medical certification requirements, aircraft departure procedures, weather conditions and communication procedures. It also includes questions regarding the private pilot duties, how to conduct pre-flight checks, landing procedures and more.

Successfully passing the knowledge exam is required for anyone seeking their private pilot license. It is a crucial step in becoming a licensed pilot — one that cannot be taken lightly.

The PPL is divided into the Single Engine Class and Multi-Engine Class. The class you receive depends on the experience of that person, as well as general aviation experience.

Although your private pilot certificate doesn't allow you to fly in commercial airspace, it does allow you to fly as a private pilot in a lower-class aircraft. In this concrete step, you'll need to demonstrate that you meet all of the prerequisites needed for each class of aircraft, before sitting down with an examiner. This is the biggest cost of the entire private pilot certification process. The checkride will cost you anywhere from $250-$1000, depending on the time of day and location. You may want to start looking at a few different flight schools with different prices. You can usually find a network of flight schools online that have lower prices that you can check out on their websites (I'll refer to this as your "price comparison group").

There is also an FAA pilot record form called a Pilot Proficiency Data Sheet (PPD-2) that you'll need to fill out. This form will give general information about your training, experience, and any health issues. You'll also need to fill this out every time you renew your training.

This checkride will be with a flight instructor from one of the schools that you're looking at. They'll go over any weaknesses or things that you may not know about your aircraft, and answer any questions or issues you may have with it. This is the biggest cost of all, as well as the most important . of the entire process. You can expect to pay anywhere from $1500-$4000 for one checkride. Once approved by an examiner, this experience will be included in your checkride.

As a student pilot, you'll be able to use the website of the FAA to calculate the time for your checkride. Let's say that you're taking a Cessna 152. The average time for a checkride in this aircraft is approximately 11–14 days. The FAA recommends that you have a minimum of 35 hours in-aircraft and 10 hours dual, with a flight instructor specifically. You'll need 5 hours solo cross country with an instructor, and 5 night training if it's required by your school. You'll also need 2 takeoffs and landings at an airport different from where you're training (by yourself), as well as 3 approaches to an airport other than where you trained. You'll also need to know all of the emergency procedures, and other various tasks that are listed in the PIL.

As mentioned before, the FAA requires that you perform this checkride before you use your newly obtained Private Pilot License to fly by yourself. This is why it's so important to meet all of the requirements beforehand and be above average in your piloting abilities, rather than simply having enough hours or flight time to take the test for your license.

The Private Pilot License certifies that you can safely and responsibly fly an aircraft around the United States by yourself. In order to get to this point, you'll need to meet several criteria that are required by the FAA. These are listed in the PIL and knowledge test (more on that later).

The Private Pilot License is divided into two classes: Single Engine and Multi-engine. Each license is further divided into three ratings: Airplane (Single & Multi), Rotorcraft-Helicopter, and Powered-Lift (helicopter only). The rating on your license dictates which type of aircraft you're allowed to operate. As for training time, to be considered for the PIL program, you'll need to log at least 60 hours of flight training. You'll also need 5 hours in a powered-lift or rotorcraft helicopter and 2 in a glider. You can do this by taking lessons in various aircraft, or you can take lessons with a flight instructor that is cross-trained.

The rating of your license depends on the type of aircraft you're taking training in. These ratings are: Airplane (Single Engine & Multi-Engine), Rotorcraft-Helicopter, and Powered-Lift (only airplanes). In order to get each rating, you'll need to demonstrate that you have an adequate level of knowledge of meteorology and aerodynamics. This will be displayed through either a Sport Pilot Rating or Private Pilot Rating, depending on your previous experience as a pilot. After you have the rating of your choice, you'll need to complete the knowledge test.

The Private Pilot Knowledge test is made up of three sections: Airplane & Power plant (FAA Knowledge Test), Knowledge for airplanes, rotorcraft & powered-lift (especially if you're taking a helicopter checkride), and Instrument Airplane (if you're taking an instrument airplane checkride). The score that is written in on your checkride report for each section will be determined by how well you did in the section. In order to pass the knowledge portion of this test, you'll need to get 80% on the checkride. Once you have the knowledge portion passed, you'll have to complete the flight training. This is where the actual license will be earned, however, it is important to remember that flight training is mandatory for ALL pilots in order to be certified by the FAA.

Pilot certificate classes are broken into two categories: Sport and Private. The class of your pilot certificate determines what type of aircraft you're allowed to operate as a private pilot.

As a Sport Pilot, you can only fly single-engine aircraft during the daytime, solo. These planes can not be faster than 120 knots (138 mph). You can not fly in controlled airspace. You are not considered to have an instrument rating.

A Private Pilot can fly any aircraft during the day, solo. They are able to fly over congested areas, and within controlled airspace. They also have a private pilot certificate with an airplane single engine or multi-engine rating. In order to get each of these ratings, you'll be tested using a knowledge test and flight test (checkride). This is what the FAA calls the Practical Test Standards (PTS). The knowledge test will display how well you've learned the requirements of your license, and the checkride will ensure that you're competent enough to fly safely at all times.

The most popular rating is the private pilot single-engine airplane. This is common because each Private Pilot License will include a Private Pilot single-engine airplane rating. If you're planning on taking a flight checkride, you should know where you stand in regard to the requirements for your license. If you're starting now out as a student pilot, and have never logged time in an aircraft before, you'll need to log at least 20 hours of flight training with a certified flight instructor. Of those 20 hours, 10 must be solo (which includes 5 at night) and 10 must be cross-country flights that take place outside of your home airport's airspace (which includes 2 landings).

As for cross-country training, you can do this by taking lessons, or you can do it with a flight instructor that has cross-training. In order to pass your checkride, you'll need to make sure to get 80% on the flight test portion of the flight test and pass the knowledge test. Whatever score is written in for your PIL (Private Pilot License) will determine what rating plane you're allowed to fly.

A Private Pilot with an Airplane rating is able to fly single -engine airplanes during daytime (24 hours) with some limitations. They are also able to fly over controlled airspace and within controlled airports under Visual Flight Rules (VFR). This can also include some controlled airspace and controlled airports that require a minimum altitude of 1,000' AGL (above ground level).

Now let's get into the knowledge in more detail. Are you ready?

STEPS TO BECOMING A PILOT

P ilots are heroes in the sky. The best about pilot careers is that despite having such a high-profile position, the responsibilities and the pay are still relatively low. For someone who loves planes, it's hard to put your finger on why you haven't yet become a pilot.

Pilots need to have many of the same characteristics that successful people have. They are independent thinkers and see things from a logical perspective. Pilots need to be rational and assess risk before taking action. They need to possess an eye for detail, accurate communication skills and be able to work under pressure.

Flying airplanes is so much more than just driving a car from point A to point B. There are tons of procedures and knowledge that you have to acquire in order to be a safe and qualified pilot. In this book, we'll go over some of the steps it takes to become a pilot, as well as the different jobs in the field once you're qualified!

If you're ready for a life-long commitment with multiple courses of study, then read on!

Most airlines require at least a Bachelor's Degree in any major, but if you're coming from a non-aviation field, it's probably difficult for them to know how well you'll do in flight school or during employment. Students with degrees in aviation related fields often have an advantage when applying for jobs.

Once you have your undergraduate degree, you'll either be required to take and pass FAA Written, Multi-Engine Training and a Private Pilot Flight Medical Exam, or you'll be able to get a Private Pilot License (PPL) and meet the minimum flight experience requirements. You can read more about the exam requirements below:

1. FAA Written Test (Knowing your stuff is key!)

This test consists of a 30 minute multiple choice test that covers general knowledge in aviation as well as sample questions covering each topic tested on your pilot's license exam. All questions are factual statements and have no right or wrong answers. The test is offered in multiple languages, so there's no need to worry about translating your answers from a language you might not be comfortable with.

The test can be found online at FAA.gov and can be taken as a separate exam, printed and brought in to take your FAA license exam, or as . of an online course.

The written test isn't required to get a job in the field, but it's certainly nice to have on your resume!

2. Private Pilot License (PPL) (Earning that License!)

If you want to make money flying, then you'll need a Private Pilot License. This license is the minimum requirement for hiring as a full time pilot. Flight training requires you to learn both classroom and flight training. You'll receive training in air law, meteorology, instrumentation, navigation and many other subjects.

Airplane-specific training will include how to manage the aircraft's controls, how to fly under different weather conditions and how to perform different maneuvers such as landing and takeoff procedures. After all your classroom and flight training is done, it's time for your checkride! This is when you'll be tested on everything you've learned throughout your studies to see if you're ready to earn your Private Pilot License!

3. FAA Flight Test (Applying for your PPL)

The flight test is the final step before earning your Private Pilot License. This test consists of a maximum of 150 questions and is based on 35 various aircraft types. The questions are all factual statements that require you to answer by selecting the correct answer from a list of options.

This test can be taken with a computer or paper based format and any pilot who has earned their PPL can take this test, regardless of current employment status or flying experience. A lot of employers look at flight test performance as an indicator for their overall ability to fly safely, so make sure to read up on the different requirements before taking it!

4. FAA Practical Test (Doing the Job)

Once you pass the test, it's time to get out there and fly! You'll need to take a two-day, 40-hour training course for each airplane you want to fly. This course is about what you've learned in your classroom training over the past few months, but this time you'll be able to practice it in the skies.

Once you finish your training course, it's off to take your practical test! At this point, there are no longer any requirements for employment and applicants are selected based on their flight performance reviews from their flight instructor. The better you perform in these exams, the more chances of being hired.

5. Initial Training (Your First Time!)

After you've been hired as a pilot, you'll continue to take formal training from your instructor. This is the type of training that's required to fly a ocular aircraft, so you'll learn each lesson and how to do it safely.

After the initial training is complete, you can start flying full time for your employer. You'll take refresher courses every three years to ensure your skills are up to date and in top condition.

These skills include:

After your initial training, you'll be able to fly both scheduled and charter flights. The major airlines have many different fleet types, so you'll be expected to know how to fly each of them before they let you go on a route.

Basic Pay

The average starting salary range for a private pilot is between $50,000 and $75,000.

On average, carriers take about 6 months to hire a pilot for their full time fleet. You can expect your first payment anywhere between two weeks and two month after you've been hired. This will include one week of vacation per year.

Even within larger cities, companies are choosing to use air travel over roadways because it's safer and more efficient. For example, larger companies like Amazon are often too big for road transportation services like UPS or FedEx.

Right now, the airline industry is in need of pilots to serve these expanding markets. Even as this industry continues to grow, there will also be a growing need for experienced pilots to mentor new hires as they come into the field.

Airline Pilot Salary by Employer

As I mentioned earlier, the employer you end up with is going to be one of the main factors in your overall starting salary. On average, regional carriers pay significantly less than major carriers and you can expect your first year's salary to be somewhere between $50,000 - $75,000 a year depending on which carrier you join. You can see an average breakdown of hourly and yearly wages below:

- Major U.S. Operated Airlines (800-900 FLIGHTS PER MONTH)
- United Airlines - $62,000 – $135,000
- Southwest Airlines - $52,000 – $128,000
- JetBlue Airways - $51,000 – $180,000
- American Airlines - $44,000 – $120,000
- Delta Air Lines - $44,300 – 119,500
- Retirement & Benefits (What you'll get!)

The type of retirement benefits that pilots can receive vary greatly depending on the company they work for and the type of retirement plan they offer. Most companies offer regular pensions that are considered a form of Social Security.

Compared to other professions, pilots have some of the best retirement plans. For example, the average retirement benefit for a new pilot with United Airlines is $3,200 per month. This amount will increase based on your yearly flying hours and pay rate during your career.

Another great benefit that most pilots receive is 'top-up' pensions. These are continuations of regular pensions offered by employers which can increase your monthly benefits if you're still working at a company that offers it. Usually this top-up pension increases with your annual bonus or salary as well.

For pilots of major airlines, this type of pension is very common. As long as you're at the company for a certain number of years, you'll continue to receive your top-up pension regardless of which employer you work for. Your pension will grow with your salary and last well into your retirement.

It's important to remember that just because you'll be getting a generous pension from your employer, it's still up to you to pay into it! . of the reason salaries are higher in this industry is because pilots are expected to contribute a good portion towards their retirement. This means that as a junior pilot, you can expect that about 5% of your paycheck will go towards your '401(k)' plan. You should also expect to make regular contributions to the plan when you're flying for the airline.

Other benefits that most pilots receive on average include:

• **Annual Leave:** Most employees get one week of vacation per year, which is capped at a maximum of 12 days per year. The lower end is around $500/week, while pilots can expect $1000/week or more depending on the amount of flight hours they fly. Pilots who fly 1-3 hours a month will receive around $600-$1200/week for vacation, while those who fly 6+ hours a day can get up to $2000/week or more!

• **Flight Discounts**: Most airlines have discount programs designed with pilots in mind. Usually the flight discounts are given to pilots who fly long-haul flights or on planes with TSA Pre-Check, but they can also include frequent fliers who have a certain amount of miles or frequent stay bonuses.

• **Flight Modifications:** Pilots can usually make any type of modification to their aircraft when it's not scheduled for regular maintenance. If a pilot wants to add extra seats, more legroom, more cargo space, etc., they'll have full autonomy to do so. The airline will often pay for these modifications as long as you have the proper training and certifications.

• **Retirement:** As I stated earlier, most major carriers offer generous pensions for pilots. The more hours you fly, the larger your pension will be.

• **Health Insurance:** Most carriers offer health insurance for their pilots, although there are some that don't offer this benefit. If health insurance is offered, it's usually around 80/20 where you'll pay 20% of premiums out of pocket and the rest will be covered by the company.

• **Cargo Insurance:** Airlines pay for all of the cargo insurance if they're already covering your flight and it's on a route they already have scheduled. This means that you won't have to worry about it!

• **Disability Insurance:** Disability insurance is rare in other professions, but many airlines offer this to their pilots in order to encourage them to fly full-time. This types of insurance will pay a portion of your income if you're disabled and unable to work.

• **Employee Assistance Programs:** Most airlines have employee assistance programs that can help you get the help you need no matter what it is. For example, they may have a program that helps you find childcare or medical benefits, financial planning, legal advice, or even workout programs!

Before you rush off and join any flight academy, there are some tips you might want to follow in order to become a pilot.

Develop Your Soft Skills

It's true that pilots don't have to be rocket scientists, but they do need to possess certain talents and skills. A pilot who is not good at this will find it difficult to get a job or will have difficulty communicating effectively with his or her co-pilots. Another important talent is to interact accurately and respond effectively in emergencies. Pilots should remember that they must always listen carefully; otherwise, they can miss cues that may indicate an emergency developing on board.

Pilots need to have soft skills such as the ability to speak clearly and express themselves clearly. They need to be able to organize themselves well - doing things in an organized manner and this will improve how they are able to organize and prepare for pilot jobs. Pilots also need excellent communications skills because during emergencies, it's essential for them to be able to communicate effectively with their passengers; however, if pilots cannot communicate properly with other people, that means that they can't effectively lead the group during emergencies.

Get Good at Math

Good math skills help pilots make decisions quickly and efficiently. It also helps them in a lot of ways outside of flying, such as while they are conducting business.

17

It will also help them keep a good flight log and make the best decisions when it comes to flying. Pilots need to be able to work well with numbers and this is one of the most important things that they can do in order to become a pilot. It's probably one of the most important skills that they must develop.

Get Your License

A pilot license is mandatory for all commercial pilots because it proves that you are worthy of going up into the air in charge of an airplane full of people. It's a sign that you are a responsible individual who will do everything you can to keep people safe.

A degree program is an excellent way to learn how to become a pilot, but it's not necessary. All pilots must have an FAA license in order to take off in the air and land your airplane back on the ground, so this is definitely where you should begin. However, if it works better for you based on your lifestyle, then by all means go ahead and earn your degree before getting a license.

Get a Job as a Flight Attendant

While you're working on getting your license, it's a good idea to do something else to support your career goals. A great way to learn is to work as a flight attendant for an airline. If you can serve passengers on the ground, you'll get some valuable experience that will help you while you are doing your training. Plus, when it comes time for them to select pilots, airlines will review the resumes of their flight attendants to see who they think is well-suited for piloting positions.

Learn How To Fly...

Learning how to fly is one of the most important things that you can do if you're going to become a pilot. A flight instructor is your best bet, because they will be able to teach you what you need to know in order to become a pilot. But it's also important for them to teach you how to learn and be responsible with what they are teaching you and it's best that they help you manage your learning process so that the knowledge will stick around.

There are some differences between flying planes and flying helicopters or airplanes. You'll find that these differences are practically negligible compared with the similarities; however, there are certain qualities that make a difference when flying both types of crafts. For instance, helicopters and airplanes both have four wheels; however, aircrafts find themselves in the air while helicopters are stationary.

You will think that you will learn everything you need to know during your first flight. This isn't necessarily the case. It's important to remember that all pilots get shaky while they are learning how to fly - and they should remember that it's going to happen because the first time you fly is the most experience you will ever have.

However, if you have a great instructor and you have confidence in them, you'll be able to get over your mental jitters and become a pilot that doesn't experience any existential angst on the first time.

All Pilots are Different

The first thing that a pilot needs to know is that all pilots are different - no two airmen are created equal. Individuals will come from different backgrounds; some will be from low-income homes while others will be wealthy. These differences create different skillsets that they bring with them. Some pilots might have better vision; others might not. The list goes on and on regarding how each individual pilot is going to become an incredible pilot who performs amazing feats throughout the skies.

The next thing a pilot needs to know is that they will be taught how to compensate for their differences. In fact, some pilots might find that they're terrible at flying, but again, all pilots are different. They will get the tools necessary to learn and it's up to them to use them and transform into something great.

...Then Become a Great Enthusiast!

There are a lot of jobs that you could potentially pursue in this line of work. Some people become pilots for the love of it, but others view it as their job. Whatever your reason for getting into this career, the sky is truly the limit!

As a pilot, you'll always be learning and growing. You must have a desire to make the world a better place, and a willingness to explore new things in the future. If you still have these qualities, then you're a great young pilot who will make an impression in this industry for generations to come.

The Next Steps...

With that, it's time to take these steps and continue on your path to becoming an amazing pilot. Next steps? Should be learning how to survive and thrive in a cockpit. You should begin researching the best schools and flight schools in your area, and then you should work on preparing yourself.

HOW TO CHOOSE THE RIGHT INSTRUCTOR

If you feel uneasy with your examiner, it is even advised to rather forgo the exam and reschedule it for later with an examiner you feel more at ease with. This may seem like an unreasonable suggestion, but it can make a difference with passing and not passing your exam.

It really comes down to your instructor. The right trainer can make you, but the wrong one can break you. Not only is this teacher responsible for instructing you about how to control the plane and manage the flight environment, but they also provide you with valuable tips for passing the exam, insight on the process, what equipment to invest in, buy secondhand or at a reduced rate, and job referrals, if you want to take your aviation pursuits further. On the other hand, if you take your training with a rather incompetent instructor or one who is unreliable, the process of acquiring your PPL will become stressful. If you decide to have lessons with the instructor, it can be a costly mistake. In fact, not only can it be a long journey but it can jeopardize the whole process of getting your FAA PPL license.

The story is heard often. The student thinks the instructor is ripping him off because he hasn't been signed off for a checkride. Student drops instructor. The student takes double the amount of instruction with a new instructor to get ready for the checkride.

Like with the instructor, if you decide to join a flight academy the school becomes a crucial component of success in getting your FAA PPL. This chapter serves to guide you on how to find an instructor that can best prepare you for your FAA PPL.

Do Research

Similar to financing your flight training, finding the best flight school or freelancing instructor involves spending time beforehand to ensure the best outcomes. With a flight school, it is slightly easier to do research. You can go online to read reviews or testimonials of previous students to come to an informed opinion of the school. Since you will also be attending a local school, phone them and ask for a tour. Tell them about your ambition to get your PPL. On the tour, visit the ground training lectures and flight training sessions to see how the instructors interact with the students. Also, consider the facilities. Are there flight simulators and other aircraft equipment? For instance, if the flight school's tuition is about $8000, but you will have access to flight simulations seven days a week and the instructors seem professional, encouraging, and knowledgeable, then you will get your money's worth from signing up with such an academy.

If you have decided to go with the freelancing instructor option, then it is more challenging to find reviews. Nonetheless, platforms where individuals advertise their services, such as on Facebook, have a comments section. It is always best to read the comments and learn as much about the instructor as possible. These are two examples of research you can do to help you to make a more informed decision. While doing research on flight schools and instructors can be tedious in the beginning, the time used is worth its weight in gold. After all, you do not want to pay about $8000 in aviation fees only to discover the flight academy is using outdated aviation regulations or poorly maintained aircraft.

Flight Instructors

In this section, we will discuss various strategies you can incorporate for finding the best flight instructor. While this may be more applicable for self-study students, if you have decided to join a flight academy with its own instructors it would also be worth your while to review this section.

Research

First, you will have to know which flight instructors are available in your area. You can go online to browse what flight instructors live in your area. Or you can go to the local air force base or aviation club and ask about instructors who work in the region. You could also join the FAA or AOPA local branch to make you better informed about what to consider in aviation instructors and who to hire. If you want to find a decent instructor, try to visit professional aviation organizations. At one of their centers, you can explain what type of instructor you are looking for and inform them about your price range. Two professional aviation organizations are The National Association of Flight Instructors (NAFI) and the other is the Society of Aviation and Flight Educators (SAFE). Professionalism and student support are considered with high regard in these associations.

Trial Lesson

A flight academy can take you on a tour, while a flight instructor can offer you a trial lesson for a reduced price. As a private teacher, I always offer potential students a trial lesson before they pay the full price. Though I lose money initially, I find that learners are more comfortable when it comes to paying for lessons after they have attended a lesson beforehand. They know what to expect. From a teacher's point of view, there are very few students – almost none – that do not sign up for more lessons after a trial. A confident and capable teacher feels comfortable offering trial lessons as they know the student will, more often than not, return.

As a prospective flight student, you know what you can expect. During the trial, you will meet your instructor, they will take you through the exercises and you might spend the second half of the lesson in the plane, where they will talk you through the flight training. Naturally, everyone has a preferred lesson style. Some students prefer more relaxed, informal approaches while others take professionalism very seriously. If you attend your trial lesson, one thing that you should keenly observe is your energy levels. Feeling tired and drained is not a good sign. Even if the instructor is passing on an abundance of knowledge to you, this too can drain you and make you lose concentration. Moreover, if you feel anxious and stressed – and you have not even stood in the radius of a plane – it might be a sign that the teacher is not for you.

Finally, not all teachers are comfortable with offering trial lessons. There are after all some risks for the instructors themselves.

Meet Different Instructors

Sometimes, after meeting one instructor you will feel confident and ready to get started. While it might sound disheartening, some instructors are good salesmen as opposed to good technicians. They will bolster your confidence in their training program and by the end of the meeting, they will have scheduled your first session. While feeling confident after the first encounter is desirable, you should also meet more flight instructors from your area. The more coaches you meet, the more informed you become about the training programs and process. You can ask more insightful questions and weigh up the pros and cons of each teacher. For example, one instructor may be a freelancer who has access to an aircraft or who works on the property at an airport, making it easy for you to arrange an aircraft and fuel. Nevertheless, you should find out about what model aircraft he has access to and what are the additional payments for using the airplane. You should also inquire as to who will be responsible for hiring and refueling the plane. Will it be included in their lesson fee or be an additional fee? Will you have to contact an airplane rental company or do they provide this service for free?

Arranging meetings with different flight teachers may delay your FAA PPL process, but ultimately it will save you money and time. This delay aids you as you will avoid switching your instructor. Switching an instructor does have its payoffs, but typically it is unfavorable. What often happens as a consequence of later switching your flight teacher, the new flying coach will require you to go through all the initial flying techniques and maneuvers to make sure that you are in fact up to scratch. The new instructor is not simply trying to make money, but they also do not want to jeopardize their professional relationship. They want to make sure you do in fact know the basics, which can use a lot of time. Thus, it is advisable to postpone scheduling your first session so that you can have at least an interview, or even a trial lesson, with different instructors before sticking with one. That said, it is recommended to stick to one, as continuity and consistency are key. If you keep changing instructors, it can make it more challenging to get comfortable with flying. The best is to find an instructor that makes learning to fly a comfortable and easy process.

How to Know If Your Instructor is a Good Fit

Below I will outline various factors you should consider when you eventually decide which instructor to go with. These points are not fixed or firmly established, but they do serve as guidelines. For example, regarding the third point, 'Full-time vs. .-time' is not a hardened rule, but it can give you some guidance.

Professionalism

There are some distinguishing hallmarks of a good flight teacher. Professionalism is one. The first sign of professionalism is punctuality. Others are reasonable rates and the manner of their feedback. Regarding the last point, if their feedback is overly critical or inappropriate, their teaching approach is unprofessional. On the second topic of reasonable rates, naturally, you do not want an instructor who is charging exorbitant fees, but you also do not want someone who is undercharging you too much, as that is also a warning light. As mentioned earlier, you do not want someone working for a cheap rate, as they feel less motivated to teach. On the other hand, you do want to balance it with a fair rate so that sessions are more affordable.

Personality

On the other hand, sometimes, it is no fault of the instructors. It can really boil down to personality. For instance, many students feel frustrated as they believe they are making slow progress. This is understandable as accumulating flight lessons becomes expensive. The instructor in this case is probably spending much time preparing for your examination, namely, going through the pre-flight inspections, aviation regulations, and procedures.

For example, once I was taking lessons with an instructor. I desperately wanted to learn the basics of flying as I had no access to a vehicle of my own. For me, the focus was first on gaining the skill of flying. However, this instructor concentrated more on me passing the exam and spent much time drilling me about the rules and regulations, which would have been fine had I been a capable flyer. In retrospect, I should have probably communicated to my teacher that I wanted to first learn how to fly as opposed to learning the rules. Though I got my license in the end, I probably should have communicated more directly about my needs. I was also young at the time.

This is an illustration that often your instructor and you have slightly different objectives based on your own circumstances. Sometimes, you can overcome these differences with good communication. Other times, you may have to resort to learning with a different instructor which makes you feel more at ease.

Full-time vs. time Instructor

This is not a hardened rule, but it can be a sign. If an instructor works full-time, they often have more expertise and can add more value to your lessons. Furthermore, these individuals can be more committed, as they depend entirely on this income and having a negative reputation can impact them immensely. Remember, if a flight instructor does this on a .-time basis, they might have various income streams. Them not being dependent on flight instruction may cause them to neglect their services. That being said, .-time instructors may love flying. They may do it simply because they receive much joy from teaching and teaching about flying.

Naturally, you can find some .-time flying coaches who have adequate expertise but are teaching .-time to complement other aviation work or to make some extra income during retirement. It is good idea to ask questions about their experience and background in aviation.

Aviation Knowledge and Lesson Structure

In aviation schools, you are more likely to work in groups, while with a freelancing instructor it will be a one-on-one session. A good instructor will be confident in both contexts and is able to deliver the content in a clear, understandable method. He or she can simplify more complex concepts for even weaker students to understand. Inflight Pilot Training expands on this, stating "They should present ideas in interesting and enjoyable ways, whether it's a lecture about instrument ratings, a hands-on lesson about flight plans, maneuver demonstrations or anything else".

Before signing up with a school and a ocular instructor or paying for bulk lessons with a freelancer, it is best to have a trial lesson or to have an interview. This will give you an idea of the teaching method and style. If you feel comfortable and the information is delivered in a comprehensible manner, it is a good sign for the future.

Other Signs

There are other aspects which you should consider when choosing a flight instructor. Check their availability and flexibility. If you are going for the self-study route, it would be advisable if you can book sessions with an instructor who will accommodate you. If they are inflexible, it might be difficult to maintain consistency and book lessons to complete your required hours. Furthermore, keep an eye out for references to manuals and guides. A flight instructor's duty is to utilize aviation manuals to prepare you for your knowledge test or to help you follow aviation regulations and procedures. Often instructors will make use of instruments, simulators, and materials to complement their studies. If there is a noticeable absence, this can also be a signal of inadequate coaching. Finally, the instructor welcomes questions and shows enthusiasm and love for flying. Also, do not be afraid to have lessons with young instructors. Sadly, there is often a prejudice against young teachers, but they are as well-equipped as any other trainer. They have also had to pass their FAA PPL and flight instruction courses. They are also generally more enthusiastic as they just have entered the profession and want to make a good impression. Therefore, pay more attention to the content of their lesson, their enthusiasm for teaching and for aviation, and the delivery of the subject matter.

Ultimately, what you want is an instructor who is professional, dedicated, and enthusiastic. Personality clashes can often create some difficulties, but they can be overcome by transparency and clearly expressing your goals. Ironically, you should be picky when it comes to choosing an instructor. In fact, the aviation industry welcomes it. Aviation associations would rather you select a teacher who makes you feel relaxed and calm than one who makes you feel edgy and anxious. This is why you can often contact the FAA, AOPA, and Inflight Pilot Training for assistance with finding the most suitable teacher.

EXPLANATION OF DIAGRAMS AND CHARTS FROM THE FAA WEBSITE

Sectional Chart Legend

Inside the airman knowledge testing supplement, which you will be given at the exam testing center, you'll find the sectional chart legend to help you during the exam. However, it's a good idea to memorize most of the icons and their descriptions. If you forget a few of them, you'll be able to reference them during the exam.

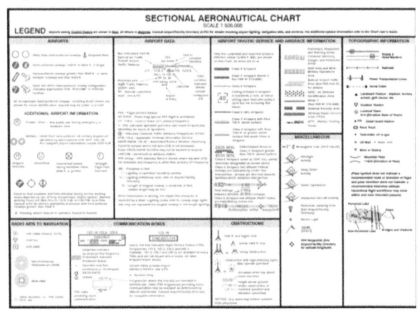

We'll be reviewing these icons as we progress through this book, and you can also download a copy of the legend. We have some icons which we'll quickly run through.

Icons and Meanings

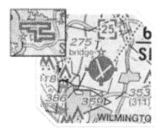

Icons indicate airports with an operating control tower. The stars indicate the airports have a beacon light operating from sunset to sunrise, and the three squares indicate the airports have fuel services.

Airports denoted in circles have runway lengths from 1500 feet to 86 feet, with an actual length of the runways stated in the aeronautical sectional chart or the chart supplement. The airport inset with just the runway icon denotes the shortest runway length, at least 8069 feet or greater.

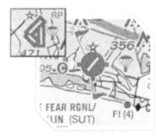

The stars indicate the airports have a beacon light operating from sunset to sunrise. The three squares indicate fuel services available at those airports. The example above is two magenta flags. Remember, it indicates VFR or visual flight rule checkpoints used by air traffic control and manned pilots for reporting points. A remote pilot in commands can expect a higher amount of manned traffic in those areas. Also shown in the icon above is a parachute icon which indicates there may be parachute jumpers in the area.

The above is another image of a non-towered airport with lighted beacon and fuel services, but the dotted circles indicate a non-directional beacon or an NDB at the airport. Also seen are a group of obstacles that are clearly labelled stacks that are 404 feet AGL. All these icons will be in the airman knowledge booklet given to you during the exam.

The image above is a group of obstacles, viable cell or broadcasting towers. The numbers on the top denote the height of the tower or structure in mean sea level, while the numbers in parentheses below show the structure's elevation above ground level or AGL.

The middle structure with the lightning bolts tells us the structure is lighted, and the tall icons depict a structure that is 1000 feet AGL or higher. The shorter icons indicate a structure that is less than 1000 feet AGL.

The image above is a group of obstacles that are under 1000 feet AGL. It is shown as the shorter icons. The lighted structure is 1029 feet MSL or 620 feet AGL. Take note of the U.C. next to the 620, which indicates the structure or tower is under construction. It clearly states the obstacles are stacks and a tower. There's also a restricted airport nearby which is denoted by R inside the magenta circle.

They are a group of wind turbines. As a remote pilot, you'd want to be aware of the presence of these turbines before scheduling any operations in the area. Also, notice the three R's in the magenta circles, which means these are restricted airports which are either private or require authorization before landing. The airport on the right is clearly labelled private PVT with the name of the airport.

Next to this non-towered airport is a glider symbol, which indicates that one can expect glider activity in the vicinity. It is where the glider is towed by a motorized aircraft. If a letter U was in place of the G, that indicates an ultralight aircraft in the vicinity. And if H was in place of G, it shows hang gliders could be expected in the area.

We have military training routes. In this example, we see VR 1667, 1617, and so forth, and again these depict military training routes where one can expect low altitude flight up to 1500 feet AGL from the surface. The four numbers indicate the altitude will be below 1500 feet AGL. The V.F. is abbreviated for VFR or Visual Flight Rules.

VR 1104 and IR 164 are military training routes, but the three numbers indicate flight training above 1500 feet AGL. The blue line labelled v289 indicates a vector flight route which is for low-level flights. They're eight miles wide divided in half, providing four miles width of flight in each direction.

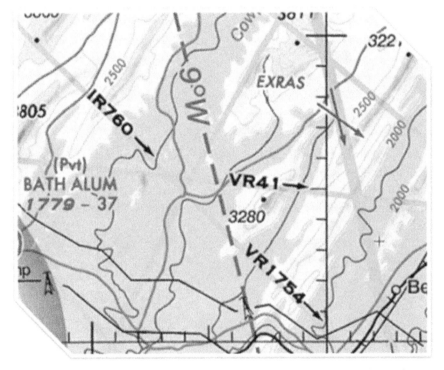

Isogonic lines are depicted as the dashed straight magenta line labeled nine degrees west. The line indicates the magnetic variation or difference between true North and magnetic North. Although we previously touched on military VFR and IFR traffic, it warrants going over again as it will likely appear on your exam.

The V.R. 41 VR 1754 and IR760 are military training routes to conduct high-speed training missions using visual flight rules or instrument flight rules.

The numbers following the letters do not depict true altitude, but rather they tell you if flights will be above 1500 feet AGL or below 1500 feet AGL. A four-digit number indicates routes at or below 1500 feet AGL, and three or fewer numbers indicate flights above 1500 AGL.

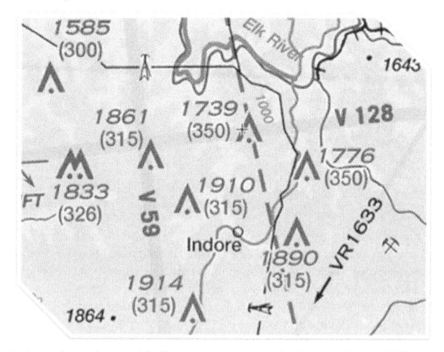

A victor airway is a straight line segment used to depict low altitude civilian air traffic. It's shown as a thick faded blue line on a sectional chart. Before now, it was depicted as black lines. You can see such on the internet. Victor airways are identified by a number similar to military VFR and IFR traffic patterns. But victor airways are always designated as class E airspace extending from a base of 1200 feet AGL up to 18000 feet MSL up to class A airspace.

The width of a victor airway extends four miles out in each direction of this center line and provides a 1000 foot clearance AGL over the highest obstacle in the area.

From the image, a few towers and obstacles are close to the victor airways that a remote pilot would need to be aware of should you be performing operations near those areas.

Airport Information

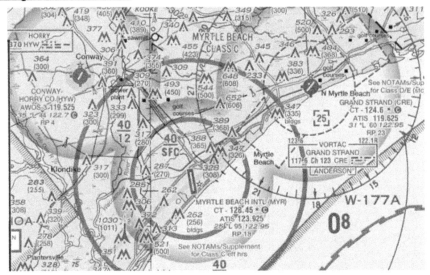

On the above is an image from an aeronautical sectional chart showing three different airports. We will be reviewing airport data information to tell us specific detailed information about each of these airports. Although the airport icons already tell us some information about the airport, the blue icon airports tell us an operational control tower. The magenta airport icon tells us there is a non-operating control tower at that airport.

But there's additional important information located next to each one of these icons. Next to myrtle beach international, you can see the information below the airport name—the ct-128.45 and so forth.

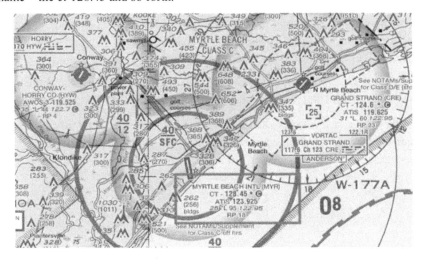

At Conway hoary, we see additional information

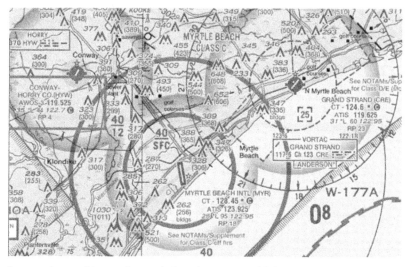

At the grand strand in north myrtle beach, we see additional airport information.

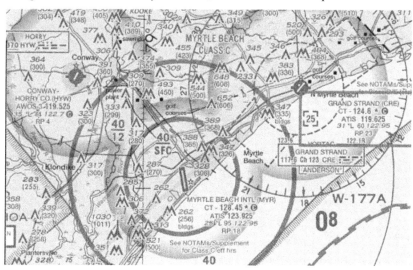

The airport data inset box, with an airport data chart inside the airmen's knowledge testing supplement, provides detailed information about each airport.

Underneath the airport name, myrtle beach, you can see ct, which stands for the control tower, and a dash with frequency 128.45, the control tower frequency.

Next to that is a star which indicates the tower is .-time, and then C inside a blue circle, which means C tap frequency. The C tap frequency is the same as the control tower frequency when the control tower is closed.

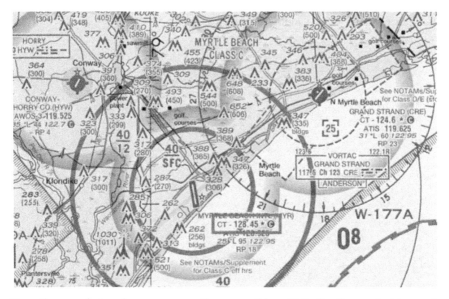

Over the grand strand, you can see the same thing. C.T. for the control tower is frequency 124.6, but it is .-time, serving as the C   -tap frequency.

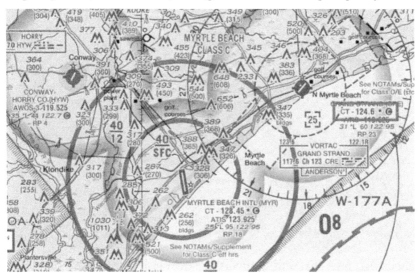

The Conway Hori, which does not have an operating control tower, has an AWS-3 frequency, automated weather observing system. Dash 3 indicates the level of services provided with that automated system. The frequency is 119.525.

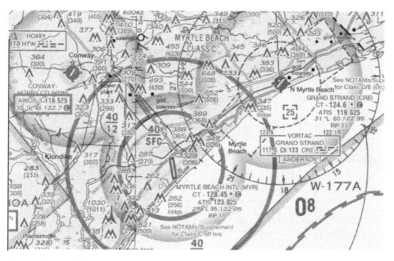

Directly underneath, as with the other two airports, you'll see some numbers. So underneath the radio frequency starting from the left, you'll see a group of numbers. The first number indicates the elevation of the airport in its actual feet Mean Sea Level. So this airport is 35 feet above sea level.

Next is a star and an L. That means there is lighting but lighting limitations. Next is a number which is the length of the runway in hundreds of feet. So the runway length is 4400 feet. A-C TAF frequency follows that pilots can tune into, which is 122.7.

The underneath of all these three airports, you'll see R.P. and a number.

Stability

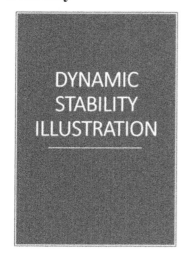 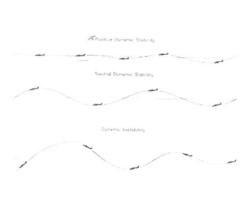

There are two things to discuss on stability. The first is maneuverability, while the second is controllability.

Maneuverability is the skill of an aircraft that permits it to be maneuvered easily and withstand its stresses.

Controllability is the skill of an aircraft to respond to the pilot control, especially in regards to the flight path and aircraft attitude. You can manipulate the airplane to where you want and achieve your result in the end. Now within the stability, there are two different things that we will discuss.

Stability is just the ability of the airplane to return or not return to its original flight path or condition after being disturbed by an outside source. So the external source could be you. You could have bumped the yoke or put the nose down momentarily, kind of inadvertently, when you're moving around the cockpit. It could also be from turbulence or what we call rough air. When you know there's a little bump, is the airplane going to remain in its same flight path, or is the flight path going to get potentially worse? I'll show you what that means.

There are two different subtypes of stability. Static stability is what the airplane is initially going to do, and dynamic stability is what it will do over some time.

So most of your training aircraft out there, like the Cessna and pipers, will usually fall in the line of positive dynamic stability. If there's a disturbance in the aircraft and you are flying straight level, naturally, it would want to return to a straight level over time.

Neutral Dynamic Stability

In neutral dynamic stability, you'll notice that the oscillations are not getting any better, and it's not getting any worse. It's riding the tide. You keep going up and down, and the wavelength is not getting taller or shorter or in any regard.

Dynamic instability

The one that's always the most challenging is going to be the dynamic instability. So let's say you bump that yolk of your aircraft and start to see oscillations getting larger and larger. That is what we would call instability. Look at this is from the screenshot below.

STABILITY FOR A PITCH DOWN DISTURBANCE

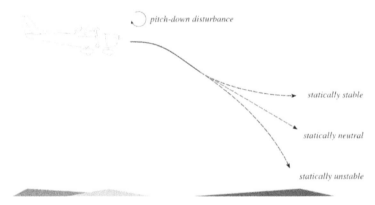

Assuming that we intentionally pitch the nose down to the Cessna, the question is, what will naturally happen with the airplane? If it was neutral, it's just going to remain in the nose-down position. If it were stable, it would try to return to some straight level, assuming that's what we were doing. If it's unstable, it's usually going to start to oscillate in the position that we don't necessarily want it to be.

So anytime we are talking specifically about an aircraft being stable or anything along those lines, it usually wants to return to its original flight condition. If it was disturbed by something, let's say turbulence or turbulent air, and it's generally going to be a bit easier to fly in those types of situations.

Engine Torque Reaction

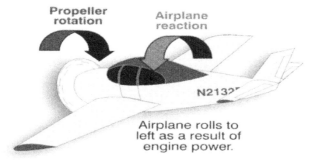

ENGINE TORQUE REACTION

Propeller rotation

Airplane reaction

N213?"

Airplane rolls to left as a result of engine power.

We have the propeller rotating from the above screenshot. When you're sitting in the cockpit looking straight out, the propeller rotates clockwise. The airplane will naturally move in the opposite direction, and it will want to roll to the left and apply more force on that left tire as you're cruising down the runway.

Now, as you do that, you will apply the opposite rudder to make this control. So the pilot will correct the yawning moment on the take-off roll by using the right rudder. So right rudder will solve this problem, and you're going to apply the right rudder in all of these cases. The amount of right rudder you use has no specific number in inches, and it all depends on the situation of the aircraft you're flying, and it's just something you learn over time. Naturally, it's one of the ways to know what to apply on our take-off and usually our climb out.

Corkscrew Effect

Another term for this which is more common, is called the slipstream effect. From the navy image above, you can see on the carrier deck; there is a spiraling slipstream. What ends up happening is that it will spiral around and eventually hit the left-hand side of that vertical stabilizer. The nose will move to the left, and the airplane's tail will move to the right when it does that. That will cause the tail to swing to the right and the nose to yaw to the left.

The slower speeds will cause the slip creams to become more compressed, and you're going to feel it to a greater degree. So when you're taking off, and you're climbing out, you're going to be at a slower airspeed traditionally, and you're going to see this slipstream effect in a greater degree than your usual.

Slipstream Effect

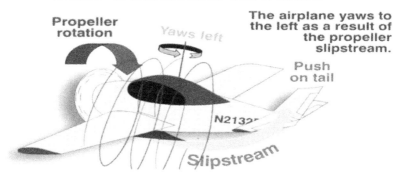

So slipstream effect is very much the same thing, and obviously, it's not coming directly from the propeller. You've got all of those kinds of eddies and currents. Eventually, it's going to push on the left-hand side of that vertical stabilizer, and as I said, the tail will go to the right, and the noses on the left, which is another left-hand turning tendency.

So it's not hard to quantify how much the effect it has on your airplane. But it will depend on your aircraft design and the phase of flight that you're currently in.

Asymmetric Loading (P- FACTOR)

It is one of the hardest for people to understand. It happens when the downward moving propeller blade takes a bigger bite of air than the upward moving blade. That occurs in two different scenarios. It's either your airplane is flying at a high angle of attack. So traditionally, if you're on your take-off or you're potentially in slow flight, meaning you are just flying slower than your usual speeds, you would have a greater angle of attack. It means that your nose is going to be slightly pointed up above the horizon.

Another scenario where the P factor is pretty common is that Pilots who learn in tail wheels or get their tailwheel endorsement will usually see this when in a tailwheel airplane. In both of that scenarios, your downward sweeping blade is at a much higher angle of attack than your upward sweeping blade. With that higher angle of attack, the downward sweeping blade creates much more of the thrust or lift in this case, and it makes your airplane want to yaw to the left. It is wordy when we discuss this, but that's the easiest way to think about it.

Always remember that with the P factor, it's primarily going to be the bite of the blade. So the downward moving blade is taking a bigger bite of air than the upward moving blade, and that's yawning the aircraft to the left under certain circumstances. When you're at a higher angle of attack, the nose is pointed slightly up.

Aerodynamic Forces in Maneuvers

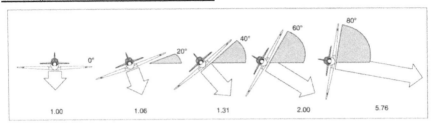

It is the load factor that some people are having problems with. In this section, I'll show you exactly how this works and how easy it is. Load factor is just the ratio of the total air load acting on the airplane to the gross weight.

Looking at the chart below, you can see different bank angles and find these numbers on your attitude indicator and flight instruments.

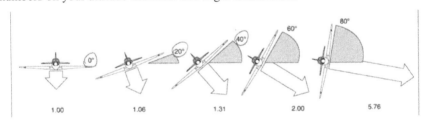

The numbers at the bottom represent G forces. So if you're straight and level, you will have 1G applied to the aircraft's weight. So if the aircraft weighs a thousand pounds with all the occupants' fuel and everything on board, 1G will be a thousand pounds. When you're in a 20° bank to the right or left, it's 1.06 Gs. For 40°, it is 1.31 Gs, and 60° is the magic number; it is 2G. So if you are in a 60° bank, that means that your wings and the aircraft have to support 2,000 pounds, even if it is momentarily. That is because it's twice the weight and twice the amount of gravity it has to keep.

You'll also notice that 60° is the magic number. So if you intentionally bank an aircraft roll or an aircraft beyond 60° right or left, or you pitch up more than 30° the nose up or down, you're required to have parachutes on board. That's one of the regulations that we're going to look at.

Once you go beyond 60°, you're going to see a pretty much exponentially sky high. You look at 80°and; you will already be at 5.76. So that's a relatively large number when we're looking at the load factor. The load factor is pretty important because you could overload the aircraft if you're not careful, and the structure can only support so much weight.

Stall Speed and Load Factor

STALL SPEED AND LOAD FACTOR

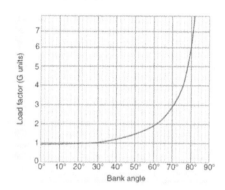

Airplanes are designed in accordance with the category system:

- Normal Category limit load factors are -1.52 G's to 3.8 G's
- Utility Category limit load factors are -1.76 G's to 4.4 G's (Mild acrobatics, including spins)
- Acrobatic Category limit load factors are -3.0 G's to 6.0 G's

When you check the pilot's operating handbook, you'll typically see three categories: Normal, Utility, and Acrobatic. Most aircraft for general aviation will at least have the Normal and the Utility.

The standard category is just generic numbers. You don't need to memorize them. It's about negative -1.52 G's to 3.8 G's.

It has a little bit larger buffer -1.7 to about 4.4. And traditionally, in specific aircraft, you can do mild aerobatics or intentional spins basically for training purposes.

There are strictly aerobatic category aircraft. These are a lot more expensive and harder to handle. You always want to get specific training when you look at it, and they are capable of far greater tolerances in terms of positive and negative G's.

You can find what your aircraft is capable of inside your pilot operating handbook or what we call an Approved Flight Manual (AFM). They are airplane versions of a car manual.

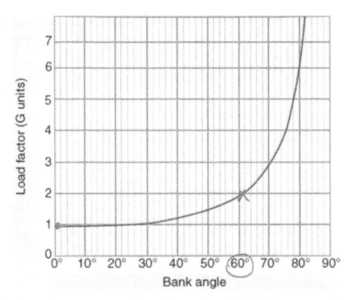

So on the chart above, we are pulling about 1G at 0°. And then, as our bank angle gets to 60, we're at about 2G's. Then like I said earlier, once you go beyond 60° and up, it is just an exponential and pretty much straight climb from there. So 60° is the magic number, and the reality is that you should not be banking beyond 45°.

For your training, you will do steep turns at 45°, and you're going to do one to the right, and one to the left during your training and check ride. Then eventually, if you get to your commercial, you do them at 50°, but no one ever really takes it intentionally to 60° when we're doing that.

Rate of turn

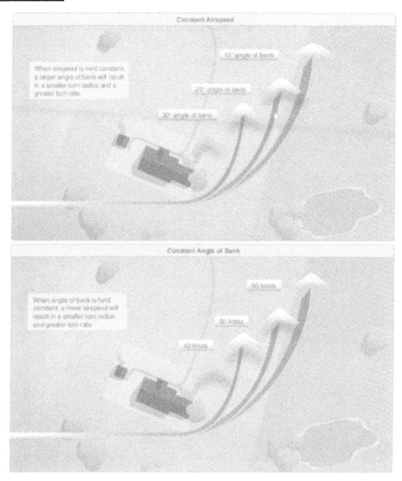

That's constantly dealing with time. So the rate is just how much time it takes. If an aircraft is flown at the same airspeed and angle of bank, the rate will be considered constant. If looking at the flying rate in the first picture, it has a constant airspeed at the top. And then, there is a continuous angle of the bank. So what we've got in the very first airplane is kind of the one on the far exterior. It is at a 10° angle, but obviously, the less you bank, the wider your turn will be.

Then if we're going to 20°, the turn is a bit closer to the house, and at 30°, we are pretty much going to pass the house as close as possible. If we look at a constant bank angle, meaning that we just bank to a specific bank, let's say 20° or 30°, then it's a function of your airspeed. So the slower you are, the tighter the turn is going to be. The faster you are going at 60 knots which is 20 knots faster than the inside, the wider the turn.

The reason why that's important is, if you were ever to get into a situation, maybe you accidentally flew into a canyon, and you realized the only way out was the same way you came in. You're coming up on a canyon wall, and you do not want to floor it as you're trying to make that turn. You want to slow down as much as possible because the slower you go, the sharper the turn you can make without taking up too much room.

Radius of Turn

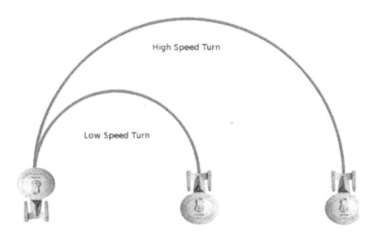

The other side on the rate of turn is our star trek side, and our radius of turn, the distance talking about the same thing as the angles.

So when we're looking at our radius of turn, and maybe at warp one with a low-speed turn, we're going to cover less distance. If we were maybe at warp ten, it goes up to that distance with a significantly wider sense of a turn.

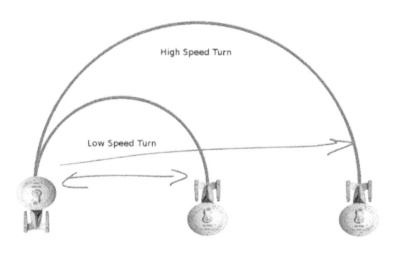

It's the same thing in a car or anything else. Suppose you've ever turned in a parking lot. In that case, you can usually make a fairly tight turn, but if you're trying to turn it at faster speeds, the turn will be significantly wider, and that's going to increase the radius of the turn.

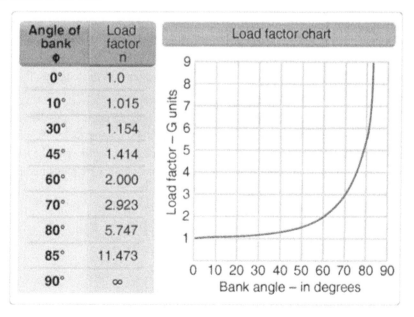

Angle of bank φ	Load factor n
0°	1.0
10°	1.015
30°	1.154
45°	1.414
60°	2.000
70°	2.923
80°	5.747
85°	11.473
90°	∞

Aircraft Engine

HORIZONTALLY OPPOSED PISTON ENGINE

In this section, we are going to discuss aircraft engines and aircraft systems. The first thing we're going to look at is the horizontally opposed-piston engine. So most aircraft out there that we deal with, except for some of the older ones, are radial engines that are a bit more complicated. All the newer engines that are piston-driven are going to be horizontally opposed.

We call them horizontally opposed because the cylinders lie horizontal, and this is a six-cylinder. So you would have a set of cylinders opposed on the other side for each one of these. The horizontally opposed engine is a pack of a lot of engines into a small little space. We will discuss the entire system of the engines like the induction system, exhaust system, etc.

The induction system is basically where the air goes into the engine, and then it gets mixed with the fuel. The other unique thing about these engines is that if we look at this cylinder, we can see one and two circled spark plugs that go into the engine. We're going to be talking about why these engines have two spark plugs mainly for safety redundancy and basically for efficiency purposes.

HORIZONTALLY
OPPOSED PISTON
ENGINE

Four-Stroke Engine

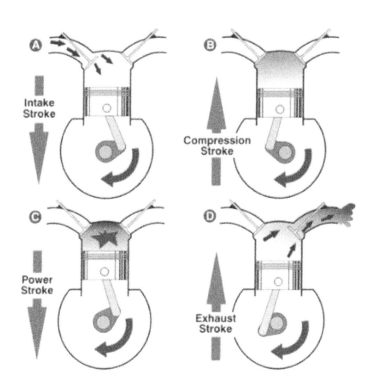

The above is a four-stroke engine. The initial stroke is an intake stroke. That is where it takes the air-fuel mixture into the cylinder. Then the second stroke is the compression stroke. The compression stroke will close the intake, and it will compress the fuel-air mixture. Then we have the ignition from the spark plug that ignites and provides the power stroke to push the cylinder back down. Then the final stroke is the exhaust stroke. That is where the exhaust is being expelled overboard outside the aircraft.

Another way for people that are less mechanically inclined is to think about the human analogy in terms of the way we eat food. So our very first thing would be the intake stroke. So fuel is going to come into your mouth. That would be your intake stroke. Then the compression stroke would be chewing the food, and your power stroke would be digestion. That would be your power stroke, and the exhaust stroke is when you undergo excretion.

Ignition System

A DUAL IGNITION SYSTEM

Dual ignition systems are installed in modern airplanes for increased safety. If the event one system fails, the other keeps the engine running.

Spark plug

Left ignition system

Right ignition system

So on the ignition system. As I pointed out before, two spark plugs deliver a spark simultaneously. Each one of these spark plugs is tied to what we call a dual ignition system. These are both linked to a magneto.

So aircraft always have a dual ignition system. There are two spark plugs per cylinder, and there are two reasons for that. The first is for efficiency, so imagine if you light a fire or generate a spark from both sides of the cylinder, it will create a smoother and uniform heat distribution. But at the end of the day, it is going to give you better engine performance. So that's the reason why we have a dual ignition system.

The secondary reason is that it increases safety. Unlike a car, we can't just pull over on the side of the road if our spark plugs decide to fail us. So if a spark plug decides not to work, we could continue operating the engine using one set of spark plugs even though we're not going to get as good performance as when we had both spark plugs firing at all times.

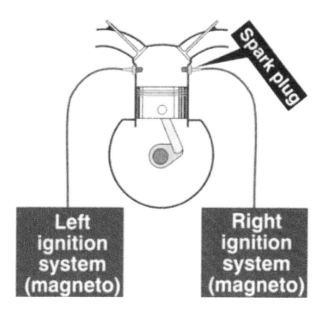

So, these spark plugs are connected to a wire, and the wire goes to the magneto. Magneto is a self-contained magnet that will provide energy, and it will deliver the electrical impulse to the spark plug while the spark plug generates the spark.

Magnetos

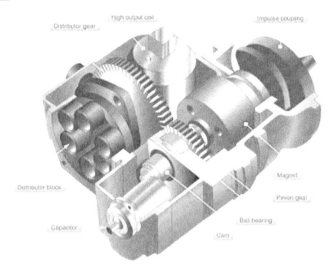

The spark generator doesn't generate the spark. If you have seen something like a distributor block, it's very similar to a spark generator, but the magneto is a complete self-contained source of electrical power. So what ends up happening is the giant magnet within this section magnet spins at very high speeds. There's a timing gear with electrical impulse sent to the distributor block. That has many wires connecting to spark plugs, which generate the spark for each cylinder. The internal magnets are spun and generate the electrical impulse for the spark plugs, and the spark is generated.

Selecting Magnetos: Cockpit View

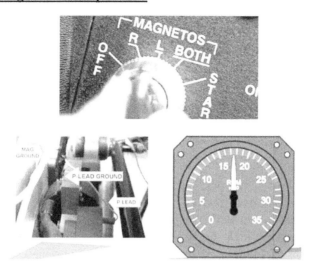

There's always going to be two magnetos and two spark plugs. The right mags will fire off a set of the spark plugs in the engine, while the left mag will fire off the other sets in the engine.

If you look by your keys, for the most., you're going to have a key with which will effectively select the magnetos on either the right side or the left side. We will always have it in both, and some are associated with a starter as well. So when we're flying in normal situations, we're always going to use both sets of spark plugs firing at all times. We have left and right because we are always going to do a run-up.

You need a check without the engine running at the beginning of the airplane or first flight lesson. You're supposed to check the flight control surfaces, check the fuel, make sure the lights work, and prepare the documents.

Once you are ready to go with your instructor, you'll start taxing, go to a designated area at the airport for a run-up. The things that we do is apply power to the engine, typically somewhere between 1800 to 2000 RPMs. Every engine has a tachometer, which is an rpm gauge, and its revolutions per minute look exactly like what you see on the right side of the image above, and we're going to do whatever the checklist tells us to do.

So if it instructs us to go 1700 or 1750, we will set the power and then run through the checklist to ask what it wants us to do, which might be to move the key from both positions. It's going to tell you to check the left mags. And what you're looking for is a drop. Traditionally the drop is somewhere between 50 and no more than though most manufacturers will specify 175 RPMs.

You're going to check it with the left and will move the key back to both. After that, you're going to check the right side, and then you're going to move it back to both for your normal flight operations. By doing this, you're checking each side of the mags and making sure the spark plugs work.

If it goes beyond a drop, that's acceptable. So if your manufacturer says that you cannot have any greater drop than 150 RPMs and you see 200, that's when you're going to go taxi it back and have a mechanic look at it. You could have a fouled spark plugs, bad spark, plugs, or your magnetos needs replacement. Those are something that usually needs to be replaced or overhauled every 500 to 1000 hours.

The other thing you're also going to notice with your mags is something called P-lead. It's a tiny wire. When selecting the right or left magneto, it's deactivating the other mag because it grounds it to the airframe. If you have that absence of a mag drop, that means the mag may be ungrounded. So this is one check that you need to do at the very end of a flight. Some instructors do it. So when you're basically done with your flight and coming in to park in your parking spot, your instructor will tell you to go off and then go to both quickly.

If you move the key off for just a second, you'll start to hear the engine wind down, and you'll move it back to both. That is because we don't like to stop the engine that way. It's not like a car. If you move it off and don't hear the engine even hesitate, that means the P-lead is bad. It's not grounded, and that's dealing with propeller safety. If it's not grounded, you're leaning against the propeller, or you're moving the propeller in the wrong direction. It can fire, and even if a cylinder fires, it makes a ail revolution. That's enough to do some severe damage to a human being. So always be cognitive if the magnetos are on and if the P-lead is working. That is something your instructor can kind of walk you through gradually moving forward.

Electrical System

In the electrical system, there is something called Avionics. There are various flight instruments in your cockpit, and avionics is where I indicated in the image below with GPS and Radio.

These are going to be powered by your batteries, so that is what's called avionics. I just want to make that clear.

Aircraft induction system

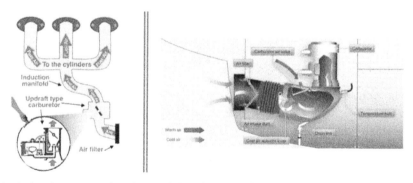

The induction system is where all the air comes into the aircraft. So there are two areas, and many students get this wrong when looking at the front of an aircraft engine. There is an engine comment that's usually open, and that is just air going in and around the engine to help cool it. Still, the engine's air goes into the induction system slightly below a couple of inches below the propeller itself. And there is an air filter that takes the cold filtered air and sends it to the carburetor.

The carburetor is the next piece of the equation that kind of sits. It is called an updraft carburetor because the air is going up, and it's being pulled up or sucked up because it's just like a venture. When we talked about aerodynamics, there's low pressure on the top and high pressure on the bottom.

The other thing that it does as well is that it has a bit trapdoor. Should the air filter be clogged entirely, maybe a bird decides to go in, or perhaps you pick up some impact ice or snow, and it completely blocks itself, that trap door will automatically open. There's nothing that the pilot will do, and it has to do with a loss of suction. It will start to suck the warm air in and around the engine comment, and that way, lost air goes to the engine.

Impact Ice

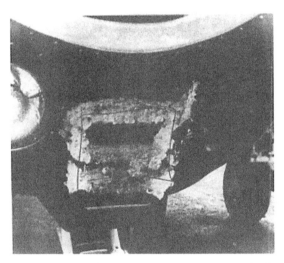

The above image explains impact ice, and by the way, the little tiny door it's your induction system. There will be a little bit of a grate on it, and that's the first layer. Then behind it lies an air filter, and that is the cold filtered air that's going into the carburetor to your engine. The other section cut off right up is the air goes in and around the engine.

That is just basically helping for cooling purposes. Now should something like impact ice kind of clog happens, the entire induction system becomes clogged. The air going in and around your engine, warmer air, will be utilized through that trap door that I showed you in the circled portion up there.

The carburetor

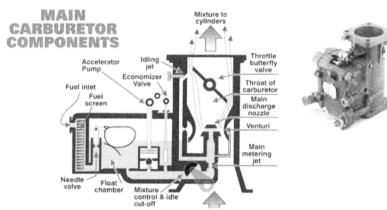

There are two different types of aircraft engines with a carburetor. The majority of the aircraft out there have a carburetor. It's just a carbureted system, and eventually, we'll talk about a fuel-injected system, mainly just the problems, and constraints. However, you still have to know about the carburetor regardless of what you fly.

So your induction system would drop the air, which ends up on the inlet below.

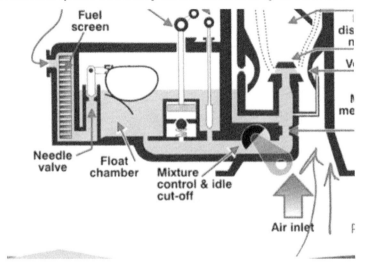

But let's talk about the carburetor as a whole. The carburetor, as I said at the very beginning, is the ultimate mix master. The top bartender, it's trying to mix the perfect amount of fuel and air in the right proportion for combustion. It will do so within the venture, which is the circled portion below.

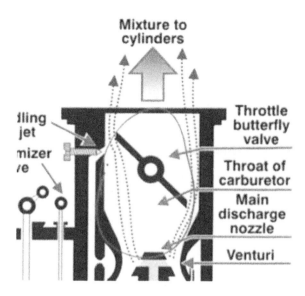

So that will send the mixture to each of the cylinders, which goes through the four-stroke engine processes discussed previously.

Fuel enters the system from its location in the wings, either the right or left tank, into a fuel screen to remove any impurities. Then it goes into the float chamber.

Everything that you see in red represents the fuel. When fuel is consumed from the float chamber, the float will go down, and when it goes down, the needle valve holding all the fuel will allow it to refill the float chamber. So that way, there's always about a gallon of fuel within the carburetor itself.

For each of these carburetor .s, like the accelerator pump, we'll go into detail and talk about what the sucker is. But at the end of the day, what will happen is that air coming in from the induction system will then go through the venture. It's shaped like a venture, and there's a narrowing in the throat. It all leads to a butterfly valve and is either going to be open or closed. The butterfly valve is associated with your throttle.

So we're going to take this step by step. What you see below is the butterfly valve for a motorcycle engine, but it works the same.

The butterfly valve on the motorcycle engine is in a closed state, so it's not allowing the fuel-air mixture to get in.

Throttle Movement & Butterfly Valve Position

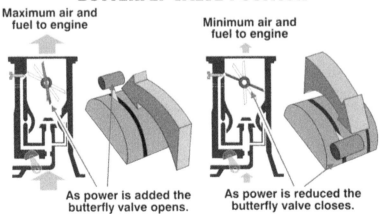

THROTTLE MOVEMENT &
BUTTERFLY VALVE POSITION

Maximum air and
fuel to engine

Minimum air and
fuel to engine

As power is added the
butterfly valve opens.

As power is reduced the
butterfly valve closes.

If you look at the image, you'll see the butterfly valve in its vertical position, fully throttled. Depending on the airplane you fly, there will always be a black handle somewhere inside your aircraft. Suppose you push the black handle away from you or towards the firewall; in that case, the power opens up the butterfly valve of your carburetor to a near-vertical position.

That will allow the max amount of fuel-air mixture to be mixed and sent to your engine, which gives you maximum power. If you pull the throttle lever back, the butterfly valve will go into a closed position, but it won't be entirely closed. That is because it's never going to be 100% closed. After all, if we closed it all the way, we're essentially going to kill the engine if we don't provide enough fuel-air mixture.

So there is an idling system that will support this. When you have no power and were to bring the throttle out, the engine will still go to an idling state, which means it will not die. That is one of the checks that we do to make sure the system is working.

There is a channel on the image below.

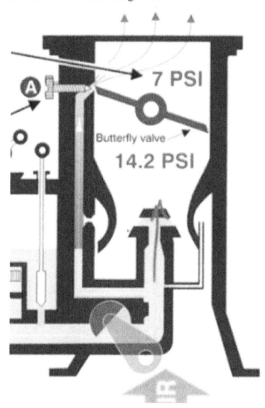

It is the main metering jet. So in the closed state, no fuel will go into the venture, but you're going to see the side channel. And what ends up happening is, it allows a minimal amount of fuel to escape from the system on the carburetor, and it's a controlled amount. There's an idle mixture adjustment that a mechanic controls.

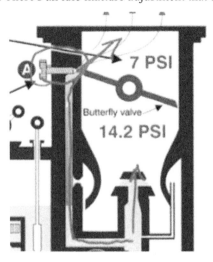

So if you were to pull the throttle out and you're doing a ground check, and your engine dies, that probably means that the tiny screw needs to be adjusted by a mechanic. You don't necessarily want to fly around with something like that. That's what allows the engine not to die when you're entirely at idle. It's a deliberate leak. That's another way of thinking about it.

Accelerator pump

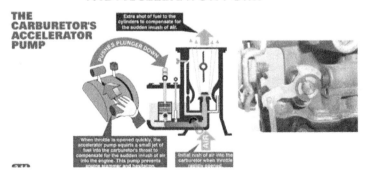

Another thing that's kind of necessary with these types of carbureted systems is an accelerator pump. Now, if you were to bring the throttle up to full slowly, the accelerator pump would not engage. If I were to smash the throttle up as fast as I could, that would push the little plunger down right below.

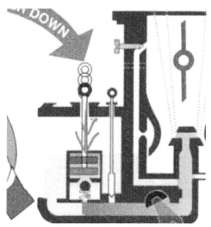

In addition, that provides an additional squirt of fuel or extra fuel pressure into the engine to give you that immediate result of increased power. That below is what the accelerator pump looks like.

We can see how small the little button is. Just realize that moving the throttle fairly rapidly because you want a rapid acceleration will engage the plunger. That accelerator pump gives it a little bit more fuel. So the engine can get going without any hesitation.

It's essential when you think about these things. You'll be asked by your flight instructor on some pre-solo exams. It's good to have a foundation of how these systems work at the end of the day. As I said before, the other thing with the venturi is, we have low and high-pressure venturi.

When we look at the image below

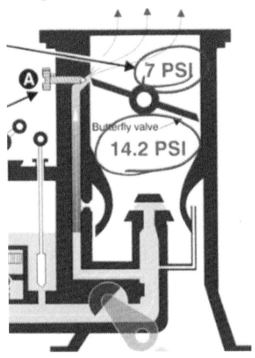

We have the high pressure on the bottom, and we have the low pressure on the top. Effectively, it's a pressure differential, just like a wing right. What ends up happening is just like a vacuum cleaner; it will try to equalize.

So all the fuel-air mixture will go from high pressure to low pressure and then be sucked up into the engine itself.

Carburator Ice

Two different types of carburetor ice will traditionally form. The temperature within the venture throat or the carburetor's throat can be about 70° colder in Fahrenheit than the outside temperatures. That is because of several reasons.

TWO FORMS OF CARBURETOR ICE

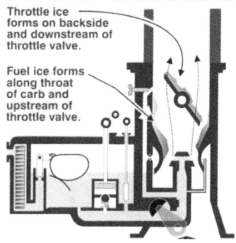

Throttle ice forms on backside and downstream of throttle valve.

Fuel ice forms along throat of carb and upstream of throttle valve.

Number one, we've got atomization. So in the little fuel jet, what ends up happening is that the fuel is atomized, which occurs for several reasons.

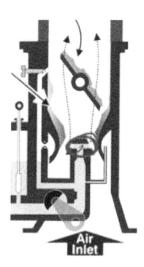

It's easier to carry the molecules to the engine and more accessible for the engine to consume fuel rather than having larger molecules. One of the problems with atomization is that it is actually like taking a spray bottle. For example, if you were to spray your face on a warm day, you would feel a bit cooler. It is what constantly occurs to the throat of the carburetor. That is where fuel ice can form, and we can start to see the red shade on both sides called fuel ice.

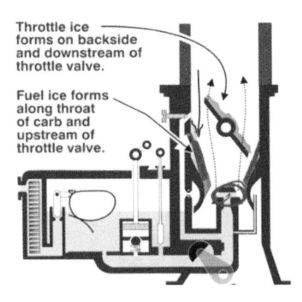

Throttle ice forms on backside and downstream of throttle valve.

Fuel ice forms along throat of carb and upstream of throttle valve.

Another thing that might occur is throttle ice. The throttle ice will most likely occur at low power or ail power, meaning not full power. Remember, if you have full power, your butterfly valve will be pretty much nearly open slightly at an angle.

If you're at ail power, you're only allowing a little bit of fuel-air mixture to enter. We start to see a bit of buildup on the backside of the throttle or the butterfly valve, which is now called throttle ice.

Critical thing to note: that carburetor ice can occur at any temperature. Some airplanes like the older Cessna 150x, 152, and some of the early 172x are well-known for carb ice. It's not an issue, and there is a way to kind of remedy the situation.

We can apply heat inside the carburetor if ice builds up, which will break it up. That heat is called carburetor heat. Keep in mind that if you let carburetor ice build up to a point, it will eventually either clog the fuel or the air inlet to the point where it will starve the engine of the fuel-air mixture, and it will kill the engine.

So it's essential to notice when that occurs and then apply the carburetor heat promptly to remove it. Another important thing is that carb ice is most likely to occur between the temperatures of 20°fahrenheit to 70° Fahrenheit, which is outside the aircraft. But it can occur at any temperature at the end of the day.

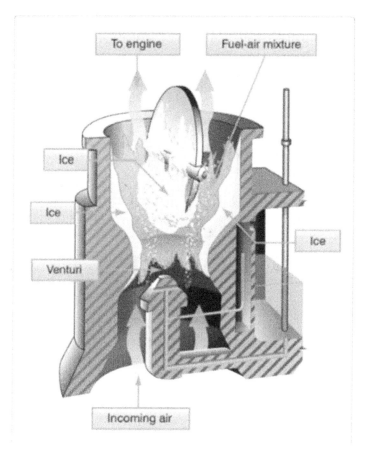

The above image is a better look at the throttle ice. So when you have a .ally opened throttle, your butterfly valve is where the carburetor ice it's most likely to happen. You're going to have a buildup of the air-fuel basically on the backside. And eventually, if you let it go, you'll see a situation where it's going to consume pretty much the majority of the throat of the carburetor. It will starve your engine of the fuel-air mixture that it needs to keep running.

The results can be alarming for pilots flying an airplane without fuel injection when the carburetor and ice come together. Carpeted racing can occur any time of the year, even on a hot day, but the most prevalent times are during cool summer and early fall days with high humidity or visible moisture in the form of haze or rain.

The venture effect of air passing through the carburetor lowers the temperature considerably, causing water vapor to freeze eventually without correction, which can cause the engine to quit.

The first sign of carburetor icing may be a slight reduction in the engine's rpm or a loss of manifold pressure. By applying carburetor heat, a flow of heated air from the exhaust melts the ice and eventually returns full power. It's necessary to adjust the mixture to smooth out the engine. So consult your flight instructor for proper usage.

If you have carburetor ice, be prepared for a further loss of power when carburetor heat is initially applied as water from the melting ice. It might be drawn into the engine, be patient, and allow the ice to melt. Power will be restored in a minute or so.

The engine may fail if the carburetor heat is turned off before the ice is completely melted. And with a cold exhaust, you won't have enough hot air to melt the ice and restore the power.

A check of the pilot's operating handbook will list the recommended times to apply carburetor heat for your ocular aircraft. Anticipate and check for carburetor icing by using carb heat periodically as an anti-icier rather than a de-ice.

Finally, be aware that the use of motor vehicle gasoline or more gas can dramatically increase the temperature range for the occurrence of carburetor icing. Carburetor ice can be fatal, but learning to recognize the signs of carburetor ice and knowing the steps to prevent it can make every flight a safe and enjoyable one.

Carburator Heater

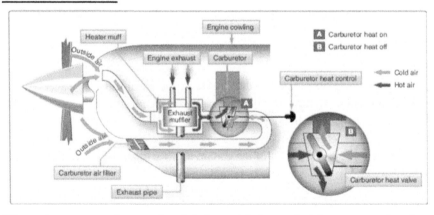

Where do we get carburetor heat? It is straightforward. After your engine four-stroke, the exhaust stroke sends all to the exhaust mufflers, which are piped outside the aircraft.

There is a metal shroud surrounding your exhaust muffler, and keep in mind the exhaust is relatively hot, but that box surrounds it. So there's outside air that circulates your exhaust muffler, which takes the radiant heat and heats the air.

You will have a carburetor heat control inside the cockpit, assuming you have a carbureted engine. All you would do is pull that out. It's going to open up the induction system that we talked about. That's going to block all the cold air because it's trying to break up ice, that will now send nice heated air to the carburetor to start breaking up and dissolve the ice, and it'll get ingested into the engine.

How to Detect Ice

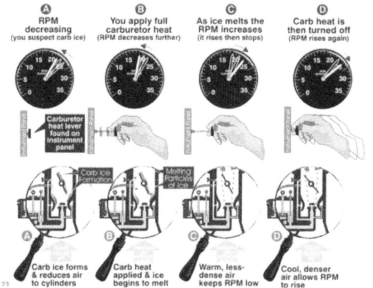

There are several different ways that we can detect carb ice. The easiest way is for some airplanes to have a carb ice temperature gauge. We do have at least a tachometer in our airplane, which is that rpm gauge, and the way we notice that we have a carburetor ice situation is that we will start to see a decrease in RPMs. We're not going to get as much engine performance because of restrictions that we can't see inside that carburetor.

From the example of the image above, we have an airplane that is basically at full power, and the airplane it's about 2500 RPMs. So at the beginning stage, you're at 2500 RPMs, doing your scan, and looking through your engine instruments. Your fuel and oil pressure all look good, and eventually, you start noticing the power is getting less and less. So this would be your first indication that you might have carburetor ice.

The pilot's going to reach over and pull out the carburetor heat to turn it on effectively. Now, as you turn it on, you'll see a further reduction of RPMs. Your engine is going to lose additional power. The reason is that the engines do not like ice and water, so they don't like to ingest them.

So you're not going to get a good performance immediately. As that ice starts to melt, the performance will begin to increase and get better. You're going to keep the carpet on, and as it starts to get better, you'll notice that it will start getting closer and closer to our goal of 2500rpm. Once it reaches the peak in which the RPMs will allow with carb heat, you're then going to push in the carburetor heat or effectively turn off the carburetor heat. You'll notice that you're going to get a bump of power back to 2500 RPMs assuming you didn't touch the power.

You're getting a bump of power because your engine likes cold filtered air. It does not like warm air, warm air is denser, and it makes your engine work a bit harder and increases air density.

The Mixture

The next thing we're going to talk about is the handle. We previously talked about the black handle's throttle, and in Cessna's, it's a push-pull in pipers. It's more like the airline-style like a throttle quadrant. The other red one in the image above is the mixture.

The mixture is essential. We don't play around with that, but we can lean the engine and get better performance and fuel savings. If you were to push in, that is called mixture rich. That is the maximum amount of fuel going to that engine. If you want to shut off the engine at the very end of a flight, you must go through the checklist.

You will notice a hand pushing the silver button from the screenshot above, which is for safety. If you want to make large movements, you're going to push that button and then push or pull. If you're going to make more fine-tune movements, you can rotate that clockwise or counterclockwise. That will move it in or out in smaller increments. You just want to be careful when using the device to make sure that you don't kill the engine inadvertently.

What controls the mixture knob is like a dam to allow you to open and control this circled portion on the image below.

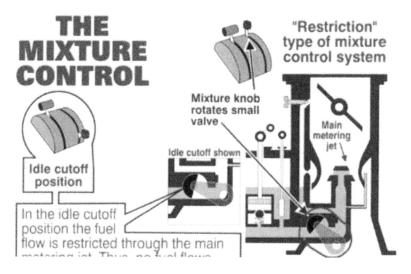

If it is mixture rich, the dam will open wide and allow the maximum fuel to go to that main metering jet. When it's closed, meaning that you entirely pull it towards you, you'll notice that it basically will act as a dam. It's not going to allow any fuel to enter the system, including the idling portion.

So basically, if that's cut off, it will cut off the idling portion and the main metering jet, which will kill the engine. So the way to remember this is, if you push it away from you or push it towards the firewall, that's basically mixture rich, or it's richer. If you pull it out towards you, that means you're leaning the engine. If not, when you pull it out, you're going to kill the engine or cut off the engine.

For the most ., we always start the engine mixture rich, and then we start to lean it for different phases of the flight. We will lean the engine for better performance and lean it for fuel savings economy. It's important to think about it where the air is much denser like the sea level. There, it will be at ten thousand feet. The air is less dense, and leaning will restrict fuel flow through the main metering jet.

VOLUME VS. WEIGHT OF THE AIR ENTERING THE CYLINDERS

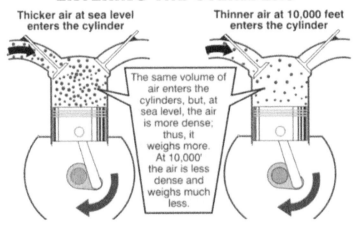

Thicker air at sea level enters the cylinder

Thinner air at 10,000 feet enters the cylinder

The same volume of air enters the cylinders, but, at sea level, the air is more dense; thus, it weighs more. At 10,000' the air is less dense and weighs much less.

Now when do you lean an engine? So anytime you increase altitude, the air becomes thinner, and it does not weigh as much for a given volume.

So to maintain the same fuel-air ratio at higher altitudes, we must manually adjust the amount of fuel leaving the carburetor. We're going to reduce the amount of fuel or lean it. So that way, it is not as rich and straightforward as when you're going to lean the engine. You always want to follow whatever the manufacturer tells you to do. That's number one or the checklist of the pilot's operating handbook.

In general, you can do it anytime you're operating at 75% power or less, any time you're above 3000 feet or want to increase your gallons per hour. So most of Cessna's out there, like the 172x, will burn about 10 gallons per hour on average. If you're running full rich, you can usually squeak that back to about six to seven gallons an hour if you're lucky. That also depends on the altitude that you're flying at.

We also traditionally lean the engine during taxis as well. There's no reason to have full rich as the maximum amount of fuel going through that engine. If we're taxing at low speeds, we're just sitting there on the ramp. Unless we take-off and at higher density altitudes such as high airports with higher altitudes like big bear or Tahoe, it tells you to ride any of these high altitude airports. For the most ., we will be taking off with mixture rich. You will learn exactly when you can and when you can't do what the tolerances are based on your aircraft.

Adjusting the mixture

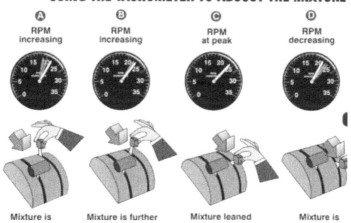

USING THE TACHOMETER TO ADJUST THE MIXTURE

Ⓐ RPM increasing   Ⓑ RPM increasing   Ⓒ RPM at peak   Ⓓ RPM decreasing

Mixture is   Mixture is further   Mixture leaned   Mixture is

These are done in different ways, and this is a little bit of an art to adjust your mixture. In the screenshot above, you'll notice that this individual is using two fingers. That is not something you want to misuse and do it rapidly in one direction or another. As I said, it is easy to kill the engine. If you brought it back and you were quick enough, you could have the engine momentarily sputter and then bring it back to life if you're fast enough. What will end up happening is, once you get to an altitude or whatever position you're at, assume that you're at full rich. What this individual is going to do is slowly start to bring it back. As you slowly begin to bring it back, you will get a bump in performance. It will increase its performance. Sometimes it will start rising to 50, 100, and 150 RPMs. As it continues to increase, you will get to what we call the peak, and the peak is the highest rpm value that you're going to get potentially.

USING THE TACHOMETER TO ADJUST THE MIXTURE

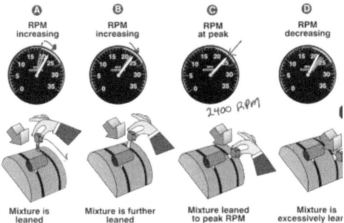

Ⓐ	Ⓑ	Ⓒ	Ⓓ
RPM increasing	RPM increasing	RPM at peak	RPM decreasing

2400 RPM

Mixture is leaned	Mixture is further leaned	Mixture leaned to peak RPM	Mixture is excessively lean

So on the image above, the peak happens to be at 2400 pm. You're going to notice that. In this case, it's about probably 60% to 50% leaned at this point. If that individual continues bringing it back, you will notice the RPMs will go in the opposite direction. That will make a mental note of where the peak is, and you're then going to enrich in it.

There are two different concepts. There's lean of peak or rich of peak. And most instructors prefer to be rich in peaks. So this means that once you get to that peak and figure out where the peak is, you will try going back to that. So if you start to see the RPMs decreasing, the individual pushes it forward about half an inch or so, which will be rich in peak.

In this way, you could effectively lean your engine using the tachometer. The tachometer is an essential instrument in the aircraft. However, there is a much more efficient way which is the EGT.

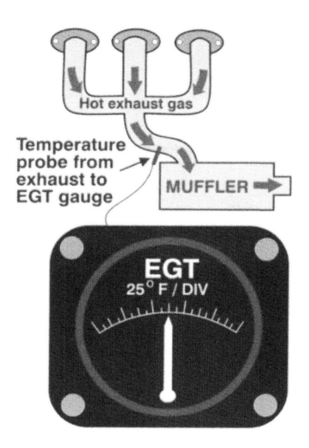

The EGT is an exhaust gas temperature. It's straightforward. It has a temperature probe before the muffle. All you're going to do is lean it the same way by pulling the mixture back and leaning the mixture. Eventually, it will get to the peak, and if you keep leaning, it will start going in the opposite direction.

Now not everybody has an EGT, but everyone has a tachometer. Then for those with the latest and greatest technology, you would use your CHTS, a cylinder head temperature. Those are temperature gauge that sits in each cylinder, and then you can lean your engine that way, and that's the best way assuming your aircraft has it, and it's the easiest way to lean.

The results are if you lean too much or potentially fly with too rich a mixture, the too rich mixture will cause engine roughness. The spark plugs can easily become fouled. If you're taxing along and you're taxing with full rich, most of your checklist, as soon as you start the engine, will tell you to lean at about 50%.

If you are moving slowly on the ground with 100 fuel going into the engine full rich, so much fuel will be sent into the cylinders, and that fuel might not be burnt off at the end. The extra amount (check image) of those lead deposits will start to build up on top of the spark plug. That fouls the spark plug and what the mechanics do is to save these. They take them out to scrape them down.

But this is also a reason why you get higher fuel consumption. If you're in the opposite court and lean too much, you will get less power. Your engine can't produce as much power as you want. It will increase the cylinder head temperatures in your engine. The image below is the cylinder.

Fouled Spark Plug

Lead deposits

That could lead to something called detonation. Detonation is an uncontrolled explosion, and this is what could result in complete damage to that cylinder.

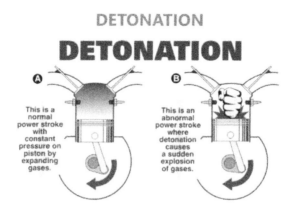

So in a normal power stroke, we usually have constant pressure on the piston by the expanding gases. We have detonation, an abnormal power stroke, which is more of a controlled explosion than an explosion caused by gas. It can damage your engine and sometimes your cylinders, as shown in the picture.

Another one is called pre-ignition. Pre-ignition occurs at a hot spot in the lead deposits between the four-stroke engine when taking a new fuel-air mixture. That lead deposit is so hot that it starts to set off a chain of reaction. The spark plug is typically supposed to engage the engine and begin to burn the fuel-air mixture. But if it does so prematurely, that's called pre-ignition. That's also not good as well.

FAA Test Question

Detonation causes in a reciprocating airplane engine when:

    A. The spark plugs are fouled or shorted out, or the wiring is defective

    B. Hotspots in the combustion chamber ignite the fuel-air mixture and advance of normal ignition

    C. The unburning charge in the cylinder explodes out instead of burning as usual.

Once again, for all those questions about lean, I will always defer to whatever the manufacturer states. Every airplane is slightly different. There are rules of thumb, and your instructors can exactly tell the mechanics of how to do that with your specific aircraft.

Therefore, detonation occurs in reciprocating aircraft engines when the unburned charge in the cylinder explodes instead of burning normally.

So, **C is the correct answer.**

AFM

A n Approved Flight Manual (AFM) is the flight crew's handbook for an aircraft type based on regulatory requirements stipulated by the aircraft's Type Certificate Data Sheet or FAA type certificate data.

It includes operational information that cannot be found in the Pilot Operating Handbook (POH), including emergency procedures, approved weights and performance data, normal takeoff distances, stall speeds, engine-out climb gradients, best climb airspeeds.

The AFM is usually produced by the manufacturer of an aircraft or authorized representative and filed with either a civil aviation authority or with the Federal Aviation Administration of United States Department of Transportation.

As an example, the Boeing 737 is certificated so that the FAA and EASA can issue a Part 23 Certificate of Airworthiness. For the type certification, and revised on 20 November 1997 (colloquially known as the 11G), it was issued as "AAXXSYO". The flight manuals for aircraft produced later than this date are identified by "AA".

For an older type certification, like A320 (colloquially known as 09G or "The Big Airbus"), it was issued as "AXXLYO", with "L" being used to mark revisions prior to November 1997.

All Nippon Airways Co. Ltd. (ANA) operates the Boeing 777. The flight manuals for the Boeing 777 (with nomenclature "AN") are issued under the responsibility of ANA-JL.

While the type certification applies to both passenger and freighter variants, ANA specifies "Flight Manuals for Passenger Aircraft with Numeric Type Certificate Numbers after 09G" for all aircraft.

The United States FAA issues aircraft flight manuals as a major part of their approval process for aircraft within their jurisdiction. A flight manual for an aircraft is one of two things: an Airplane Flight Manual (AFM), or an Airworthiness Limitations and Alterations (ALAM) document. Although very similar in nature, these two documents serve two very different purposes.

Aircraft flight manuals are developed for each specific airplane design which is manufactured. This is done to establish a complete set of limitations and procedures for the operation of the aircraft as originally designed. The AFM is bound in hard-copy form, and is not changed based on any future alterations or alterations approved by the FAA Airworthiness Branch during the lifetime of that aircraft design. Changes to an airplane design are handled through Airworthiness Limitations and Alterations (ALAM) documentation procedures published in Advisory Circular 21-65C, dated October 23, 2011. The ALAM document establishes a separate document number which supersede previous versions of that specific type design. For example, an aircraft that has had changes to the design after its original production may have a new version of its AFM unless the FAA requires further changes. In this case, a new Airworthiness Limitation and Alterations (ALAM) document would be issued in addition to the new version of the AFM.

The ALAM document is marked with the effective date of the change it applies to, and is not intended to establish a life limit on an aircraft operating under a previous version. The AFM, if not superseded by an ALAM for that specific type design, will remain in force until an appropriate alteration or amendment is accepted by the FAA Airworthiness Branch. In practice, this means that an airplane may need to be operated under two or three separate documents through its airworthiness life. Airworthiness limitations and alterations documents are usually issued as a result of changes in regulatory requirements, accidents and incidents, or the introduction of a new design feature. Changes to an AFM are not accepted by the FAA Airworthiness Branch, and are handled by the manufacturer of the product being changed. These changes include anything from mechanical changes to approved operating procedures (although many of these procedures will be documented in the AFM for future use).

On 20 November 1997, Boeing's certification for their 737-600 was amended so it could be identified by "AA" for up through 737-700 series aircraft. The flight manuals for later Boeing 737 types have been identified by "AA", including the 737-800.

There are restrictions on the number of pages that can be contained in a particular type of flight manual. For 737 aircraft, the AFM may not exceed 42 single-sided pages printed on 8 1/2 x 11 inch paper in letter size format (21 x 29 cm). Older models like the DC-10 and 727, with nomenclature "A", were limited to 30 pages per model. The Airbus A320 family has a 66 page limitation. Some airliner manufacturers like Bombardier specify an even larger number of pages allowed per model type.

There is no internationally standard format for flight manuals. However, the use of SAE AS5553 is common in the aerospace industry. The United States Federal Aviation Administration (FAA) specifies the use of Standard Form 825-90, "Standard Formats for Aeronautical Information Publications", which describes a number of formats used by the FAA to organize their publications. The body of an AFM typically contains all of the following information: Some manufacturers may not include some items, or may include additional items which are unique to their product design. The AAC, for example, contains the following items:

The AFM also contains a number of amendments to previous versions of the document. These are noted by a "9" or "1" in front of the revision date. If a specific version of the AFM has been superseded by an ALAM (as described above), the ALAM will have an asterisk (star) before it in place of that number. Some manufacturers may provide you with airworthiness data or maintenance manuals, which are audited and approved by their respective regulatory authority.

Some airworthiness data and maintenance manuals are only available to pilots and flight engineers, although maintenance manuals are often available to mechanics and engineers.

USEFUL INSTRUCTIONS FOR PPL STUDENTS

The FAA PPL is, without doubt, a difficult course. This is not only because it includes theoretical and practical components. You will also need to master flying capabilities and apply what you have learned from simulation sessions. Overall, you will need to dedicate much time to studying and developing your flying capabilities. Whether you decide to take the course part-time or full-time, you will still need to make many sacrifices throughout the duration of the FAA PPL course.

During groundwork, simulations, and practice flights you will need to concentrate on the instructions and procedures. Finally, you will need to be committed to the course even outside course hours. This includes reviewing course material and making sure to book your flight lessons in advance so that you can be guaranteed consistent practice.

While the last chapter aimed to provide you with a brief outline of the FAA PPL course, this section will go into much more detail. It will help you to apply for the course, learn about each section of the course, manage your time effectively during each stage, and eventually, prepare for your final exam. Thus, we will analyze the various sections of the FAA PPL such as groundwork, weather analysis, simulations and flight sessions, and aviation terminology. Once you are familiar with what each stage involves, different tips and guidelines will be given to help you pass to the next one, and finally to get you to the examination itself.

While it may feel daunting, as there is a lot of information to absorb, procedures to memorize, and capabilities to master, this guide aims to provide you with step-by-step instructions for obtaining your license.

Application for the FAA PPL Course y Student Pilot Certificate

The Student Pilot Certificate is an official document that declares you are a student in training to obtain your Private Pilot License. It allows you to have lessons with a nationally certified flight academy and to practice flying following the guidelines of the certified flight school. To obtain the Student Pilot Certificate, you need to apply for one from a District Officer or from a flight school.

Before you complete your application form or choose your flight school, you need to select the type of plane. As with motorcars, motorcycles, and trucks, there are different licenses and certificates for different classes of vehicles. Generally, with the FAA PPL you will start off in a Cessna 172. The Cessna 172 is an airplane. There are different aircraft classes, such as gyroplanes, balloons, gliders, and helicopters, and different requirements and regulations for each aircraft class. Before filling in your application form, check out the local flight schools to see if they have the class of aircraft available for your practice sessions. For an airplane, you need to be 16 years old, while for a balloon or glider you need to be 14 years and older. As mentioned earlier, you will also need to be able to speak, read, write, and listen in English to be accepted for the program. Once the above are all in order, you can move onto completing the application form. For in-person forms, you can submit them to an instructor at your flight school, or you can send them to the Flight Standards District Office (FSDO). If you have been successful at locating a flight school, it is important that you submit your application with a part 141 flight school or an instructor who has the correct certifications.

Once again, make sure the teacher is certified for the relevant aircraft class. Initially, it is necessary to make sure you cover all these bases, as you do not want your application to be rejected on the grounds of incorrect aircraft class or to have an administration mistake moments before you take your FAA PPL exam. If all your details are correct, it will take about three weeks for the District Office to process your application and send your Student Pilot Certificate.

The good news is that generally there is no charge for the student pilot certificate. However, if you ask your flight school instructor to apply on your behalf, there may be a fee from the school. When you attain your FAA Private Pilot License, you will hand in your Student Pilot License.

Medical Certificate

During this time, you will also need to obtain your medical certificate. You can generally apply at the Aviation Medical Examiners (AME) for your medical certificate. There are two steps for this process. First, you must fill out an application, either on the website of the FAA or AME. Next, you will have to make an appointment with an Aviation Medical Examiner, who will conduct the medical check with you. Once you get the medical examiner's approval and you have received your student pilot certificate, you can begin your flight school course. It is best to check with the AME regarding new medical policies. For example, some high-risk groups may face some restrictions with obtaining a medical certificate. Therefore, when scheduling your appointment with an Aviation Medical Examiner, ask about any updates to the latest medical regulations with the FAA and AME.

While it might go without saying, aviation is strict on testing for drugs and alcohol. Regarding the former, you will fail your medical certificate if you test positive for such substances. This is true for pilots working in both public and private enterprises. Furthermore, for your PPL you will need to get a third-class medical certificate. For commercial pilots, they will need to obtain a first or second-class medical certificate. With first and second-class certificates, they need to be renewed every six months and twelve months, respectively, while for your PPL and third-class medical certificate, it only needs to be renewed after two years.

There are some debilitating health conditions that prevent an individual from acquiring any class of medical certificate or can cause their medical certificate to become non-valid. These include epilepsy, having a permanent pacemaker, a heart transplant or testing positive for substance abuse as already mentioned above. The FAA has to ensure that safety, even at an individual level, is always a priority. Therefore, some individuals with chronic health conditions may not receive their medical certificates on that basis. For the medical certificate, the AME fees are from about $80 – $150. Like with your Student Pilot License, you will need to present the medical certificate during all of your practice flight sessions. If you fail to have the documents with you, you will lose the class. So, to avoid any disappointments, it is best to come to class prepared with the necessary documentation.

The FAA PPL Course and Exam

Upon getting your medical certificate and student pilot certificate, you are now ready to attend the FAA PPL course and begin flying lessons. Your principal goal is to pass the FAA Private Pilot Checkride License Exam. There are two parts to the exam. First, you will need to pass the written or theory test, an oral test, and finally your check ride. Flying Academy offers the course full-time in a period of two months. Training programs with other flight schools can be three months. If you cannot attend full-time, most schools offer a part-time option. If you take the training program part-time, the course can be extended from four months to six months.

The FAA PPL Course

The FAA PPL is an intensive training program. There are three main steps you need to follow before you can obtain your Private Pilot License. In this section, we will discuss each section, your main goal for each stage, and guidelines for completing the section. While flight schools compile the various sections into a training program and schedule, one can complete all three sections without enlisting into a flight academy.

Step 1: Groundwork and Flying Practice Sessions

Groundwork, or Ground Training, is composed of all the theoretical education you will cover. Pilot Institute explains the nature of Ground Training, In ground school, you learn the theory about how airplanes fly, meteorology and weather conditions, airspace, FAA regulations, and other aviation topics. The objective of ground school is to get you to pass the knowledge test and equip you with enough theoretical knowledge for the practical aspects of flying. For Part 141, you will have to complete 35 hours of Groundwork. Most flight academies divide groundwork into three stages. After each stage, you will have a written exam. On passing the exam, you will move onto the second stage. This may differ from flight school to flight school, so this may not apply to your local academy.

In Step One, your main goal is to complete the 35 hours of Ground Training so that you can be adequately prepared for the theoretical test. On completing every module and hour, your instructor at the flight academy will sign your logbook detailing how many hours of content you have covered.

It is best to try to absorb as much information, and remember key content, as you can since you will be tested on them later in Step Two for the theoretical test, which will be discussed below. Furthermore, revision of notes is key to quickly grasping the concepts, learning the terminology, and familiarizing yourself with the regulations. First, asking questions stimulates the brain, as opposed to simply giving up on understanding. If you do not understand, but continuously are trying to figure out a solution, this forces your brain to come up with a solution and to make connections. Thus, if you cannot understand something or solve a problem, it is best to keep at it (at least twice, if you have limited time), and to make sure you go to your instruction for the solution or answer.

Groundwork (Home-study course)

For those aspiring pilots who have decided to skip flight school and take lessons with a freelancing instructor, you will also need to complete the written test. Unlike flight academy students who attend lecture-style lessons, you will need to self-study. In this case, you can ask your freelancing instructor for the various materials needed to pass the written exam. As you cannot attend classes, you will need to approach your freelancing instructor with proof of your groundwork self-studying. The instructor will sign a logbook declaring that you have covered the necessary course material. On completion of your 35 hours of groundwork, you can apply to take the written exam at an FAA testing center.

Flight Training

At the same time as your Ground Training, aspiring pilots will also have to complete Flight Training. While some Part 61 schools are more flexible about the required hours of Ground Training – Part 141 schools are more rigid with the number of Groundwork Hours – both Part 61 and 141 flight academies are more inflexible with the required hours of Flight Training. You will need to complete some hours flying with an instructor and flying solo. They are different for Part 61 and Part 141 schools.

Like with Groundwork, Flight Training is also divided into three sections. With Part 141 schools, you will need to do 35 hours of practice flying as a minimum, while a minimum of 40 hours is required for Part 61 schools. In addition, for Part 141 schools, you will also need to conduct one solo flight which is a minimum of 5 hours in length, and you will also need to pilot another cross-country dual at night. On the other hand, for Part 61 schools, you have to complete a solo flight of a minimum of 10 hours and also complete a nighttime cross-country dual. In both schools, you also need to make sure your solo flights are 50 NM (Nautical Miles) and 100 NM. It is also required of you to have one night fly. These are the general requirements for both schools.

The three stages of Flight Training total 30 hours of flying practice. In the sessions, the instructor will teach you basic techniques, landings, take-offs, and protocols for emergency situations. In total, you are required to spend 25 hours on the fundamentals of Flight Training. You will also learn about cross-country navigation in these lessons. On cross-country navigation, you will spend approximately 5 hours in training. There is no difference here between the Part 141 and Part 61 schools.

For the next part, you will engage in solo flights. During solo flight lessons, you will be flying the plane, but under the guidance and supervision of an instructor. Naturally, if you have completed the number of hours with an instructor and they believe you are capable of solo flights, you can move onto this area. For solo flights, Part 141 schools require that you complete 5 hours of solo flights. On one trip, you will need to land at two different airports (excluding the departure airport) and fly 100 NM. Part 61 schools need students to complete 10 hours of flight training. Once again, students on one trip have to land at two different airports (excluding the departure airport) and also travel 100NM.

If you wish to skip flight school and hire a freelance instructor, you will also need them to complete your logbook showing the above details: the number of hours you have completed with an instructor and on solo flights. The instructor will also need to make the judgment on whether you are ready for the practical exam. Once you have completed the necessary hours and the instructor has given you the thumbs up, you can proceed to the second and third steps. Your principal objective with Flight

Training is, therefore, to complete the 25 hours of aviation fundamentals, the 5 hours of navigation and from there to either do a 5-hour solo flight for the Part 141 school or a 10-hour solo flight for the Part 61 school. The best way to accomplish this is to utilize your practice sessions as much as you can. Your instructors are not simply supervisors or chaperones, they are vessels of knowledge. Using their full wealth of knowledge and requesting their opinions or support can immensely contribute to your learning. While it may sound a bit abrupt to say it, you are paying them for the service of teaching you.

Flight Training (Self-study course)

Self-studying students will need to hire an instructor for the Flight Training. Like with the academy instructors, freelancing pilot coaches will introduce basic flying maneuvers, take-offs, landing, and navigation. One of the upsides of self-study is that with freelancing instructors you can apply for more lessons and enjoy greater flexibility which works around your schedule. Nevertheless, much of the responsibility will lie on the student to arrange times and to follow up on issues they are having with flying techniques.

Another responsibility that lies with both the student and freelancing instructor is to complete your logbook.

Step 2: Pass the Theoretical Examination

After Ground Training and Flight Training, your main goal is to pass the three-stage exams which compose the Theoretical Examination. You will be awarded your Student Pilot Knowledge Test on completing the theoretical tests. You will need to get a score of 70% to pass the written test. Additionally, on the day of the exam, you will bring your identity card. It should be noted that different aviation schools have varying testing methods. Some include a three-stage examination process, while others require you to only take one written test. In the case of three exams, it is mandatory to pass all three. Nonetheless, it may seem less stressful to only have one exam, but it also entails having more to remember. Therefore, it may be a better option to attend an institute where you have to take the written test in three stages

The first stage can be considered an introduction to aviation, aerodynamics, airplanes, communication, and flight environment. After you complete these sections, you will need to complete the Stage 1 Exam. On passing your Stage 1 Exam, students will then cover meteorology (weather analysis), Federal Aviation regulations, and Pre Solo Exam. You will also study navigation and airplane performance. Next, you will attend the Stage 2 Exam. Like with the Stage 1 Exam, if you pass this second exam you can move on to the final section. The last area of groundwork includes cross-country flying and human factor principles. Finally, you will be ready to take the Stage 3 Exam. Once completing the groundwork discourse and passing the three exams, you can move on to Step 2, provided that you have covered the Flight Training section. Some schools differ in their approaches to the theoretical exam. While many learners aim only to get the minimum 70% score for their written test, this can backfire on them. The theoretical exam also influences the result of the final step, the checkride. Shawn Hardin is a commercial pilot and professional aviation instructor. He, like myself, has many years of experience in the industry, and now provides aspiring students with the FAA PPL preparation. Hardin also reveals that aiming for a 70% could potentially result in failure. You may just fail the paper. Then, you will be required to pay for a repeat. If you have to retake too many times, it could get pretty expensive.

A good tip Hardin provides is to take the written test as early as possible. Once you have covered your 35 hours of Ground Training, do the exam. The knowledge is still fresh and you can get it out of the way as soon as possible so you can concentrate on Flight Training. Once you finish the theoretical exam, for the next two years your certificate is valid. You have ample time to passing your checkride in a confident manner. In the final two chapters, I will list the most essential aviation terminology and cover past paper exams to best prepare you for the FAA PPL written and oral test.

Step 3: Pass the Checkride

The checkride is your practical exam which is also the final test you have at the end of your Ground and Flight Training. It involves the oral part, we spoke about above. While checkride is the more commonplace term, to avoid any confusion, it is referred to as the practical test. Once you have finished your oral, you will need to plan a cross-country flight. Next, the student will have to conduct the trip as per the plan. Finally, the examiner will reveal to the student if they have passed or not. On passing, the student will receive their Private Pilot License (PPL). Before you can start the test, you will have to show the examiner the necessary documentation, such as your student pilot license, medical certificate, national ID, and logbook. It is also recommended to have a backup in the form of a hard copy so that nothing prevents you from taking the test on the day. You will also need to pay a fee of $350 to $500, which you need on the day of your exam. If an instructor is accompanying you, there will also be a separate fee for the instructor. If you are attending a flight academy, you will need to check with the school if an additional fee is required on the day. It is advised to prepare all of these in advance and include backup documentation. You do not want to have to reschedule your test.

Oral Section

During the oral segment, you will have to answer questions related to the theoretical components, such as flying procedures, pilot documentation, and aviation regulations. For example, the examiner can ask you questions about whether you are a legal aviator or not, about the differences between a pilot and student license, and about your medical certificate and condition. After these routine questions, the examiner will ask you about aircraft systems. The student will then have to draft a cross-country plan. The cross-country plan also forms part of the oral section. You will be questioned on airspace during the departure and arrival, communication, and weather conditions.

The Flight Exam

The practical exam consists of a weather briefing and then a preflight inspection. You will start your cross-country flight. The term cross-country flight is a bit misleading as people generally do not complete the journey.

The examiner will introduce a flight obstacle. It can be a situation of engine failure or a diversion to make an emergency landing for the nearest hospital. In this case, you are being tested on procedures during an emergency. Before you land, the examiner will bring in a new challenge, like an unexpected vehicle or animal on the runway. If you are able to fly smoothly during the first two waypoints, follow the instructions, integrate the necessary procedures during the emergency and diversion, and not make any erratic maneuvers, you should pass the exam. Upon completion of the test, the test taker will tell you directly that you have passed or failed.

Moreover, if you fail you will generally be informed on what exact area was your weakness. If you pass, the examiner will complete the necessary documentation and you will have obtained your PPL.

The best tip you can get for your practical exam is to relax. While it is certainly easier said than done, if you are not relaxed, you can jeopardize a positive outcome. For instance, the examiner needs to feel comfortable with you. If he is apprehensive and dreading an accident, this will impact you passing your license. Furthermore, being relaxed also has a practical element. If you are uptight and nervous, your body is more constricted and less flexible. It will be more difficult for you to implement flight maneuvers or control the vehicle. Your taut frame will make it difficult to steer the plane and it will become a jerky ride. While it might sound odd or counterintuitive, if you do not feel comfortable with the examiner, then it is better to reschedule. The last thing you want is to feel nervous, stressed, or apprehensive during your checkride - the practical exam.

Reschedule your flight if you cannot feel at ease with the examiner. While it may seem like an extreme resolution, it is probably safer and more guaranteed of being successful in the long run.

In the last two chapters, we will focus on preparing you for the final exams. Chapter Seven will give you a list of the essential aviation terminology to help aspiring pilots become familiar with aviation industrial language. The final chapter will provide you with past papers listing questions generally asked in the written and oral exams. These chapters both hope to adequately prepare you for your FAA PPL license.

FAA PPL Course Preparation

The most cost-effective way to approach the FAA PPL checkride license is to be well-prepared. It will be more cost-effective because you will spend less money on retakes. First, you need to know what to expect. This chapter has outlined what the FAA PPL course will look like. As you know what the program entails, you can choose how to manage your time. Naturally, you will first have to decide about part-time or full-time training or if you should go for a self-study option.

Being well-prepared is not only more cost-effective and increases the likelihood of success, but it also aids in stress management. If you leave studying for the last minute, you will be overwhelmed with information. In terms of flying, we have already discussed how being relaxed is crucial to succeeding on the day of the practical exam. This is not only true for the big day, but for every day of flight training. When you are prepared, you know your procedures and aerodynamics. However, if you feel overwhelmed because you cannot recall the above, you will feel more and more stressed during the flight and worse during an emergency.

In addition, if you can spend less time fretting about what procedure applies to which conditions, you can concentrate more on the task at hand. For instance, if you are in a flight training session, you do not want to be distracted by trying to remember aviation regulations and aircraft systems. Therefore, preparation allows you to focus more and assimilate more knowledge. Another way to prepare is to optimize your time now. Like the reading you are doing now – which is a way of preparing for the process – you can begin your studying now. What I mean is do not begin your Ground Training now – and certainly not the Flight Training – but use this time to learn more about the structure or format of the different exams. This can slowly make you more familiar with the process and mentally prepare you for the day. Also, if you have decided on whether to go for the part-time or full-time option, try to come up with a schedule that can allow you to manage your FAA PPL studies and other commitments. Having other commitments – especially time with friends and family – can help you to relax and enjoy the process more. After all, it is three to six months of training.

If I could do my FAA PPL again, I would use the processing time of my Student Pilot Certificate to do more research and do some pre-studying. For example, it is recommended to study basic aerodynamics and weather principles and practice in flight simulators before beginning your training or even applying for your Student Pilot License. The simulators can give you a feel for the experience while going through the content can help you to know what is expected. In fact, eighty percent of flight school students drop out. While there are various reasons responsible for this, two of them are a lack of structured training and unclear goals. Lack of vision and unstructured training are two things which you have influence over now before you have even started your course. This chapter specifically has dealt with the FAA PPL training program. You can start creating your goals and schedule for the course now.

Finally, the best thing is to get started as soon as possible. While COVID-19 has impacted the aviation industry, it is largely the commercial or public aviation sector which has been negatively affected. The private industry is booming. As there are many social distancing regulations for commercial flights, governments and business personnel are resorting to private air travel to circumvent COVID-19 restrictions. Furthermore, this is good news for those who are opting for self-study. More instructors and schools are putting their content online, thereby making the process more affordable and flexible. It can be concluded that the aviation industry has not been extinguished during COVID-19, but rather it has shifted from the commercial to the private. Therefore, if you are looking to become a pilot, as counterintuitive as it sounds, now is the best time to do so.

Despite ending the last section on a positive note, the FAA PPL course is no Sunday picnic. It is hard work and requires much commitment. Whether you study online or through an academy, the road to obtaining your license will not be free of obstacles. For instance, while both Part 141 and Part 61 schools require you to take 35 hours of flight training, generally you will need about 60 hours of flight training. This is one illustration of how it is much easier to write down step-by-step instructions, but in reality, it is an immensely difficult process. That is why approximately 80% of flight school students abandon the course. It is, by no means, easy.

That said, this chapter has sought to provide an overall outline of the FAA PPL schedule and program, and to give some tips to better prepare you for the course, bearing in mind that it is immensely challenging and necessitates having a high level of commitment. I would like to emphasize the preparation, dedicating yourself to one task at a time, and making informed and practical decisions about how to go about the course are essential to attaining a successful outcome in a practical exam. I end on a positive note. The private industry is booming now. There is a real motivation and is now sensical to become a non-commercial pilot. Despite the immense suffering and overwhelming amount of information to absorb, there are others who have succeeded in the past, and their knowledge they have passed down to us can help us to smoothly walk in their shoes. Now that you know what the FAA PPL course entails, you can make an informed decision about whether flight school is really for you.

CFI

To become a Private Pilot in the USA, or any country which uses the FAA's standards of training, you need to pass two tests: The Private Pilot Knowledge and Airmanship Test (PK-A), and the FAA practical test for Private Pilots (PTP). These are taken in sequence at a CFI accredited CFI school. Once you have passed these tests, your instructor will give you an endorsement letter and sign off on your logbook as qualified to fly solo as a private pilot. For a CFI to sign off on or endorse a logbook, you must take every step in his or her due diligence, as outlined in the Uniform Logbook Guidance Notes. In addition to completing the course of study with the CFI and successfully completing the PK-A and PTP tests, you must also complete a recurrent training with your CFI. This recurrent training is an additional pre-requisite for the CFI endorsement required for the logbook endorsement. This recurrent training e minster consist of a one-hour class review and two to three flights of 2 times 30 minutes within 90 days."

"To complete your license, you also need to pass a checkride with an FAA instructor at an FAA regional office in your area."

"The Training Course: You will study one section at a time in the same order as outlined here. You may study from your book alone or in combination with the website and the DVD. The website and DVD contain extra information, including audio presentations of the theory, video demonstrations, and interactive features that let you evaluate what you have learned."

"The FAA Practical Test (checkride): This will take place at a designated FSDO located in your area. To schedule your checkride, call the number provided above."

"The FAA recommends that you take a CFI Checkride within 60 days of logging 6 solo hours to ensure that you retain all you have learned."

IACRA Registry (International Aviation Registry) is an electronic database of more than 436,000 pilots and their records. Each pilot's record contains information such as the pilot's license, medical certificate and airman documents. IACRA enables pilots to submit applications and supporting documents to the FAA, as well as manage their records and print certificates. Applications and petitions may be submitted via web forms on the IACRA website.

In addition to pilot records, the system also manages records for certain aircraft registration numbers and medical examiner certificates.

The Registry was first implemented in 1967 using mainframe computers at FAA Headquarters in Washington DC. It was originally known as "FAA/AIMS" (FAA Aviation Information Management System). In 1992 it was renamed "AIS/AIMS". In 2002 it became "IACRA".

In June 2010, IACRA was selected as the standard for managing pilot certificates in the United Kingdom.

A specific type of CFI is defined by the FAA for some aircraft. The following are types of CFI: This list does not include all CFI, but is only a small sample. For more information about each one, see their own article or visit the FAA's site.

The English Wikipedia currently has the most detailed and up to date article on CFI with the current changes from that point of view. A few visitors have noted that some of the included entries are interesting, while others use a lot of misleading or incorrect information.

What are the contents of CFI in Private Pilot Lesson?

During CFI you will learn the Checklists for general certification requirements, Aviation databases and resources and you will take some FAA knowledge tests. You will also have some books, those are: A pilot's operating handbook for small aircraft - Aircraft finance guide and The Flight Manuals of the different types of aircraft in Kontact Aerosport, Inc. fleet. This includes the Cessna 172, Cirrus SR20, Pilatus PC12/45 and Saab 340B. You will be able to develop aeronautical decision-making, improve your Flight preparation for VFR flight over water or mountain operations, including use of checklists, your Flight planning, learn all the Safety precautions for flight, Weather-related information, Emergency procedures (how to operate the aircraft and its systems in an emergency),Fault isolation and troubleshooting techniques. It includes techniques for a student to become an independent pilot.

You will become an expert about Weather briefing, weather data and forecasts, including wind conditions, visibility, clearance delivery procedures, mountain areas, mountain/water use charts and special weather advisories/warnings.

You will do some Flight training lessons. This includes general aviation topics such as flight performance (powerplant characteristics), flight planning (flight profiles), instrument approach procedures; aerodynamics(flight controls) etc. These include FAA approved materials (Flight Training Manuals) and use Radio communication and navigation equipment.

You will deal with ATC services and facilities, METAR, TAF, and NOSIG reports, IFR flight plan filing procedures. This includes information on STARs and SIDs in CFI in Private Pilot Lesson.

Also, with IFR navigation techniques using VOR (radial/DME or ADF) or GPS. This includes a variety of IFR procedures, including holding patterns, course reversal, Standard Terminal Arrival (STAR), DME arcs; airways, radar vectors, etc. These include FAA approved materials (Flight Training Manuals) and ILS approaches and landings, Traffic patterns (straight in, overhead and offset) over the runway. This includes pattern altitudes, traffic conflicts, etc. Other than Crosswind take offs and landing.

You will learn about Specific / unusual airport operations including practice with night flying, Departure procedures (clearing the airport on various runways). This includes various types of departure procedures, including VFR and IFR. This includes a variety of techniques such as low/high altitude VFR departures;

departures over water; using the Jeppesen departure procedure; etc. These include FAA approved materials (Flight Training Manuals), Night flying, GPS ground procedures. This includes DME arcs and intersections.

You will have some Flight training lessons that cover the different types of weather conditions, including visibility limits; cloud layers; icing regions, etc. These include FAA approved materials (Flight Training Manuals).

Lessons about Airspace rules and regulations regarding VFR flight, the Use of the Jeppesen approach plates in CFI in Private Pilot Lesson, ATC communications and radio navigation systems, Collision avoidance through recognition of traffic and airspace position awareness techniques. This includes the identification of traffic using sight, sound; by transponder replies to ATC calls. These include FAA approved materials (Flight Training Manuals).

You will know Principles of instrument flight, Instrument landing system (ILS), Instrument procedures, Navigation systems, including VOR, NDB and GPS. This includes ground procedures for GPS approaches, GPS holding patterns, GPS airways and DME arcs. These include FAA approved materials (Flight Training Manuals), DME arcs, GPS approach procedures. This includes GPS waypoints; RNAV (GPS) approaches; localizer back course approaches and different types of GPS approaches. These include FAA approved materials (Flight Training Manuals).

Also, ATC services, Aircraft performance data and limitations. It includes performance data for take-off and landing distances, climb, drag and fuel consumption for all aircraft in Kontact Aerosport Inc.'s fleet. It includes VFR, IFR and crosswind climb rates for all aircraft flown in CFI in Private Pilot Lesson, Operational techniques and procedures, including use of the charts, flight planning and the FMS.

You will deal with Training flight, on our fleet of aircraft, Aviation databases and resources, Aircraft finance guide, Aeronautical decision-making and Operational techniques and procedures, including use of the charts, flight planning and the FMS.

Training flight

This section includes a walk through of checklists for flight preparation, preflight check, during flight: engine failure on short final; engine failure after V1; engine failure in level flight; wind shear; stalls (wing down and power off); spins (recovery from spinning); low altitude air turn back procedure.

You will go through Airplane performance and limitations, VFR regulations, Collision avoidance, Air traffic control systems, Airport environment, including ground operations and parking.

You will learn how to use the charts to prepare for flight. This section includes a walk through of the selected charts (airway magenta, blue, red and outer ring charts) and procedures that can be used on these charts.

Also,Joint Flight Plan (JFP),Terminal Doppler Radar (TDWR) reports,IFR flight plan filing procedures. This section includes information on preparing for and filing an IFR flight plan, including DME arcs, VOR radial distances, NDB bearings and frequencies. This includes a variety of techniques such as: filing at other airports than the one at which you normally operate; filing low altitude VFR plans; using Jeppesen's FMS; etc. These include FAA approved materials (Flight Training Manuals).

You will learn everything about Night flying,Departure procedures (clearing the airport on various runways). This includes VFR departures; low altitude IFR departures; airway, out of area, crossing and radar vectors. This includes a variety of techniques such as: filing low altitude VFR plans; using Jeppesen's FMS; etc. These include FAA approved materials (Flight Training Manuals).

Also,Weather conditions and flight planning, Flight planning procedures with charts. This section includes procedures for flying over the ocean, mountain ranges, approach charts and holding patterns, STARs, DME arcs; approaches to airports/runways/runup areas. This includes a variety of techniques such as: filing at other airports than the one at which you normally operate; filing low altitude VFR plans; using Jeppesen's FMS; etc. These include FAA approved materials (Flight Training Manuals) and Ground procedures. This includes the following information for our fleet of aircraft; VFR airport diagrams and procedures (including holding patterns), DME arcs, VOR radial distances and frequencies, NDB bearings and frequencies, GPS approach charts and GPS waypoints, GPS hold charts. This includes a variety of techniques such as: filing at other airports than the one at which you normally operate; filing low altitude VFR plans; using Jeppesen's FMS; etc. These include FAA approved materials (Flight Training Manuals).

You will learn Principles of instrument flight,Instrument approach procedures and use of the Jeppesen approach plates in CFI in Private Pilot Lesson, Air traffic control services, Collision avoidance through recognition of airspace position awareness techniques. This includes the identification of traffic using sight, sound; by transponder replies to ATC calls. These include FAA approved materials (Flight Training Manuals).

Also, Training flight on an approach chart that comes with our fleet of aircraft, Airport environment, including ground operations and parking, how to use the charts to prepare for flight. This section includes precautions for night flying; nocturnal navigation; and parallel runways. This includes a variety of techniques such as: filing at other airports than the one at which you normally operate; filing low altitude

VFR plans; using Jeppesen's FMS; etc. These include FAA approved materials (Flight Training Manuals).

You will study how to operate in mountainous regions; airways and holding patterns. This includes operating in mountainous areas, airways and holding patterns. This includes using the charts, including a section on the various types of terrain that may require special use of the flight crew's judgement. This includes a variety of techniques such as: filing at other airports than the one at which you normally operate; filing low altitude VFR plans; using Jeppesen's FMS; etc. These include FAA approved materials (Flight Training Manuals).

TERMS & DEFINITIONS, ACRONYMS & ABBREVIATIONS

Though it is often overlooked, communication is fundamental for flying. Clear communication between ATC and a pilot can be the difference between a safe and risky landing. Epic Flight Academy provides more insight on why thorough knowledge of English is essential for pilots and ATC. As successful flights depend on communication between pilots and ATCs, much of flight training is dedicated to aviation terminology and industrial language. However, as the above quote reveals, there are hundreds of terms. This poses a great challenge to student pilots as they need to become familiar with many acronyms, phrases, and words in a short space of time. Some of them are familiar enough such as 'mayday' and 'ATC'.

However, some have been misunderstood over time such as 'roger' which means to 'acknowledge but not necessarily comply'. Furthermore, terms or words take on a new meaning. For example, a taxi in aviation language is completely different from a private vehicle that you can rent to take you from one place to another. In this sense, mastering aviation language can entail relearning definitions and becoming familiar with odd compound words such as Zulu time. As an aviator, I recognize the immense difficulty in becoming fluent in aviation industrial language. Thus, this chapter aims to provide you with a list of basic aviation terminology and their definitions to best prepare. Lastly, it is essential to study from the updated list of aviation terminology. Therefore, if you choose to use other sources or handbooks for your exam preparation, make sure that they are using current definitions.

Aviation Terminology and Definitions

Before getting started with the lists of terms and definitions, I would like to explain the approach of this section.

Various terms will be grouped under headings such as 'maneuvers' so that it is easy to understand the expression, and it becomes easier to remember it as you associate it with other similar phrases. Other manuals have different approaches. They usually offer an alphabetical list – which can work effectively for some learners – however, it can be a bit overwhelming.

The Basics

You need to learn the Radiotelephony Spelling Alphabet, also known as the NATO phonetic alphabet. The words which compose this list are unique so in emergency situations, even if you are stressed, they will not be confused for other words.

- A: Alpha
- B: Bravo
- C: Charlie
- D: Delta
- E: Echo
- F: Foxtrot
- G: Golf
- H: Hotel
- I: India
- J: Juliett
- K: Kilo
- L: Lima
- M: Mike
- N: November
- O: Oscar
- P: Papa
- Q: Quebec
- R: Romeo
- S: Sierra
- T: Tango
- U: Uniform
- V: Victor
- W: Whiskey
- X: X-ray
- Y: Yankee
- Z: Zulu

- **Abort:** This can refer to any previously planned maneuver. For example, if a pilot cancels a take-off or a landing, it is an aborted take-off or landing. Naturally, this can be an instruction from ATC, or it can be communicated to ATC in the event of canceling a planned maneuver.
- **Absolute Altitude:** The absolute altitude is the distance from the aircraft to the ground in a vertical line.
- **Absolute Ceiling:** When the plane reaches the highest altitude it can on a climb or ascent, this is called the absolute ceiling.
- **Accelerated Stall:** Compare with 'stall'. An accelerated stall happens when the airspeed is at a higher rate than the load factor.
- **Adiabatic Lapse Rate:** As the altitude increases so does the temperature decrease, this is known as the 'Adiabatic Lapse Rate'. Similarly, with decreasing altitude the temperature begins to increase
- **Adverse Yaw:** When the drag on the wind becomes too much, the nose of the plane turns in the opposite direction. This is an undesirable consequence called the Adverse Yaw.
- **Aeronautical Information Manual:** This is a guide that provides guidelines on appropriate and official pilot operation or conduct according

to the FAA, aviation safety regulations, and the rules of the US National Airspace Safety.

- **Affirmative:** Yes. This is generally as a response to verification questions. For example, if ATC is confirming your amount of fuel, a pilot uses affirmative to state that is in fact correct. Please refer to 'Negative', 'Roger', and 'Wilco' below.

- **AGL (Above Ground Level):** You will see this abbreviation come up a lot in the next section. This refers to the distance measured vertically between the land and the aircraft.

- **AIM (Aeronautical Information Manual):** This is an easy abbreviation to remember. AIM refers to the Aeronautical Information Manual, which contains the latest regulations from the National Airspace System, Air Traffic Control (ATC), acceptable conduct of a pilot, and aviation safety rules.

- **Airfoil:** The airfoil is what you see from a cross-section diagram of a plane: the wing, propeller blade, rotor, and sail. To simplify, if you look at the plane lengthwise, from its nose to tail, you have a cross-section of the plane.

- **Aileron**: On the wings, each side has a hinged-control surface which works with the roll motion of the aircraft.

- **AIRMET (Airmen's Meteorological Information):** An on-flight advisor provides the pilot with weather conditions or forecasted weather conditions in the context of the pilot's capabilities, the status of the plane (fuel or weight of the aircraft), and aircraft equipment to help the pilot better manage the weather conditions.

- **Airport Indicator:** This is a code composed of three letters assigned to each airport so that it becomes easily distinguishable. For example, LHR is London Heathrow Airport, JFK is John F. Kennedy International Airport in New York, FRA is Frankfurt International Airport, and CDG is Paris Charles de Gaulle Airport.

- **Airspace**: Airspace – which differs from aerospace – is one of the most complicated concepts of aviation as it deals with rules and classes. There are five classes, Class A, B, C, D, and E. Each has different visual rules which apply, and some are generally busier than others. There is also a Class G, but this is considered uncontrolled airspace. Nevertheless, rules still apply to this zone.

- **Airspace Classes:** See the above comment on 'airspace'. Airspace class refers to a specific section of atmosphere. The National Airspace System lists different rules for each class, Classes A, B, C, D, and E. You should also study 'controlled airspace' and 'uncontrolled airspace'.

- Note: *For the FAA PPL exam you will have to learn about the different rules which govern each class. In the next chapter, we will cover questions about airspace.*

- **AMT (Aviation Maintenance Technician):** This is the abbreviation for an aircraft mechanic or someone who repairs the aircraft.

- **Angle of Attack:** This deals with geometry and vectors. The angle between the airfoil and the direction of the air colliding with the airfoil.

- **Approach:** There are a number of terms which include the word 'approach'. The term 'approach' specifically refers to a pilot's intention to land at an airport. However, Skybrary explains how 'approach' is used in a specific context.

- **Approach Clearance:** When ATC has permitted you to approach or land at acicular runaway at a certain time, they will give you an 'approach clearance'.

- **Approach Gate:** This is one of the final instructions as ATC provides. Once the plane has made contact with the ground, ATC indicates which gate will be the final destination of the plane.

- **Final Approach:** This is when the aircraft initiates a path in direction of the runway which ends with a landing.

- Approach Speed: The necessary or recommended speed for the landing is 'approach speed'. Over the course of the landing, the altitude and distance will differ throughout the landing.

- **Arrival Time:** This one is generally known to all. This is when the aircraft will arrive on the runway after a flight.

- **ASI**: Airspeed Indicator refers to an instrument which works out the airspeed of the plane or aircraft. While it depends on the country, airspeed is calculated in miles or kilometers per hour or knots.

- **ATC:** Air Traffic Control or Air Traffic Controls which is either the system of communication between airport towers and pilots or the individuals who perform this function to safely navigate all flights at an airport.

- **Altimeter:** Altimeter is the instrument which indicates the altitude of the aircraft.

- **Angle of attack:** is somewhat complex. Epic Flight Academy provides an exact definition, "The angle between a reference line on an airfoil and the direction of the oncoming air". While the angle of attack can seem similar to the angle of the nose of the plane towards oncoming air or wind, it is calculated to the reference line of the airfoil. You should also refer to the above 'airfoil' to better understand this concept.

- **Apron:** A designated paved area for an aircraft to unload or load, and for it to receive fuel.
- **ATIS** (Automatic Terminal Information Service).
- **AWIS** (Aviation Weather Information Service).
- **Back Taxi (Backtrack):** Also refer to 'taxi'. For back taxi, this usually occurs pre-take-off. The aircraft is moving on the runway but remains on the ground. As opposed to 'taxi', the aircraft heads in the opposite direction to the one in which it will take off or land.
- **Base Leg:** When a plane begins its descent in the direction of the runway in preparation for landing.
- **Blade Angle:** The blade angle refers to the angle between the line of a propeller blade and the rotation.
- **Blind Transmission:** See 'Blocked'. This relates to radio communication. When a blind transmission occurs, two-way communication cannot be formed. This does not happen due to interference, as the broadcast is received. Nevertheless, the pilot and ATC are not able to communicate.
- **Blocked:** This strictly refers to radio transmission. When the transmission has been blocked, it means that there has been some disruption or interference with the communication perhaps owing to several broadcasts occurring at the same time.
- **Cabin Crew**: Most passengers are familiar with cabin crew. Cabin crew are the workers of an airline who work with the pilot to ensure safety protocols are followed during the flight.
- **Calibrated Air:** This is the corrected airspeed that is adjusted or corrected by an instrument's reading.
- **Cargo**: This one is simple enough. 'Cargo' are the goods carried and stored onboard during the flight.
- **Ceiling**: The 'ceiling' is when you reach the lowest cloud. As clouds can obscure a pilot's ability to see, this term 'ceiling' is essential.
- **CFI**: A CFI is a certificate for a flight instructor. Naturally, when choosing your flight instructor is it essential that they have such a qualification.
- **Circle to Runway:** This is an instruction from ATC to tell the pilot that they will need to make a circle to execute a landing.
- **Clear Prop:** Before the pilot turns on the engine, he or she will have to inform the ground staff and ATC that the engine is going to start running and that the propellor will begin turning.
- **Clearance:** When ATC authorizes a maneuver, this is known as a 'clearance'. Below, we will consider various types of clearances.

- **Cleared as Filed:** This is the clearance given for a flight plan. After the aircraft has been assessed and confirmed as airworthy, it receives clearance for the flight plan. This is known as Cleared as Filed. Even though the aircraft is authorized for the flight plan, clearances for take-offs, altitude, DP, DP transmission, and landings will have to be individually given permission by ATC.
- **Cleared For Take-off:** Once the conditions – terrain, weather, and runway traffic – are known, ATC authorizes an aircraft with permission to de..
- **Cleared to Land:** This one is straightforward. After the airspace conditions and runway traffic is verified by ATC, an authorization to land is given.
- **Clearance Void If Not Off By (Time):** Heathrow is once again the perfect example. Since there are two minutes between landings and take-offs, there is limited time for aircraft to act. An aircraft has to execute a maneuver within a specified time. ATC has provided clearance for that time frame, but the pilot needs to act within that time frame. If the pilot fails to perform the maneuver, they will need to receive another clearance.
- **Climb**: When the plane increases altitude or goes up, it is called 'climb'.
- **Climb to VFR**: This involves knowledge of Airspace. When proceeding from one Class to the next, ATC authorizes the aircraft for the ascent. VFR refers to the Visual Flight Rules for each class. As the weather conditions differ, there will be different VFR to ensure that the pilot is able to see within each class. For more information, see 'Visual Flight Rules'.
- **Cockpit**: The 'cockpit' is a generally known term. It is the front of the plane where the pilot sits and where the pilot panel is located.
- **CofA** (Certificate of airworthiness). Each aircraft will not be permitted to fly without one. This shows that an aircraft is equipped with the necessary aviation systems to meet the current FARS (Federal Aviation Regulations).
- **Commercial Pilot:** This refers to anyone who can receive a payment or a salary for aviation services. When you first pass your FAA PPL, you will be a private pilot and are able to fly to where you desire. However, only when you are a certified commercial pilot can you make money from flying.
- **Comply With Restrictions:** ATC will explain the altitude and speed restrictions to the pilot for upcoming arrival or de.ure. This term is normally used to indicate that the pilot will follow the restrictions.
- **Contact Approach**: CTI pft, an aviation website, explains that there are two types of flight plans, one which follows VFR (see VFR and see Airspace) and IFR (see IFR). When certain visual conditions occur – for instance, the pilot's field of vision is free from clouds – and the plane is

one mile away from a destination, the pilot may choose to follow VFR instead of IFR.

- **Continue**: This is another instruction which is given allowing the pilot to proceed with the current maneuver either a descent or taxiing.
- **Controlled Airspace:** For more information, also refer to Airspace. In controlled airspace, the pilot is required to follow all instructions provided by ATC.
- **Convective SIGMET**: As mentioned earlier, a weather advisory provides a report of current and forecasted weather conditions. Convective SIGMET are warnings of weather conditions which include thunderstorms, tornadoes, and generally intense weather conditions. Also, see 'Air met' and '' …
- **Course Deviation Indicator (CDI)** – The CDI is an instrument indicating when the plane is not completely on course.
- **Cross (Fix) at (Altitude):** When ATC establishes a new altitude restriction, this is known as Cross (Fix) at (Altitude). For example, ATC provides instruction on what altitude restrictions apply. There are a number of similar instructions which ATC requires pilots to comply with. These include Cross (Fix) at or above (altitude) and Cross (Fix) at or below (altitude) (Pilot/Controller Glossary, 2018).
- **Crosswind**: For landings, crosswinds pose a great challenge. A crosswind intersects the course or direction of the aircraft, making any maneuver more difficult to execute.
- **Cruise**: Abiding within IFR, ATC provides clearance allowing the pilot to maintain their speed at a specific altitude. The Pilot/Controller Glossary explains this term in more detail.
- **DA (Density Altitude):** Density altitude considers the air pressure of a specific altitude above sea level.
- **Delay Indefinite (Reason if Known Expect Further Clearance Time):** Either ATC uses this term to indicate that a delay is to be expected or that the duration of the delay is unknown. For instance, if the weather conditions make a landing impossible, ATC will not be able to give the pilot an expected time for the delayed landing. ATC, in this case, might recommend a landing attempt, but the pilot will have to remain on standby for the next step from ATC.
- **Descend**: This is the opposite of 'climb'. When the plane loses altitude or goes down, aviation terminology defines this as 'descend'.
- **Deure Clearance**: As you will begin to notice, there are a number of clearances which ATC has to give for you to proceed with the flight. To conduct a demure, ATC will communicate a demure clearance.

- **Deviations**: This refers to maneuvers which do not comply with instructions provided by ATC. In specific weather conditions, a pilot deviates from ATC instruction. In such instances, ATC may allow pilots this liberty as the conditions do necessitate such deviation.
- **Direct**: A direct is a direct line between two navigational aids or points or waypoints. Once again, using your sectional charts, when planning your flight plan you will refer to certain measurements as straights, the ones which follow a direct course.
- **Distance Measuring Equipment (DME):** This is another type of instrument which calculates the distance from the aircraft to the ground station.
- **Distress**: See Emergency.
- **Dogfight**: This is an aviation term for air combat; two aircraft engage in combat or fight.
- **Downwind Leg:** This refers to flying parallel to the runway, but in the opposite direction from the direction of landing. This is flown at a specified traffic pattern altitude generally a half-mile to a mile from the runway.
- **DUATS** (Direct User Access Terminal Service)
- **ETA** (Estimated Time of Arrival)
- **ETD** (Estimated Time of De.ure)
- **ETE** (Estimated Time En Route): This term refers to the total time spent traveling to the destination.
- **Elevator**: This is a control surface on the horizontal axis which works with the pitch of the aircraft. Also, refer to 'Ailerons' and 'Tailplane'.
- **Emergency**: This one is clear. It is a signal of distress or urgency.
- **Empennage**: This is the tail of the plane.
- **Execute Missed Approach:** To fully understand this term, you will need to know what is meant by a Missed Approach. See Missed Approach for more detail.
- **Expect (altitude) at (time) or (fix):** In the case of communication failure, ATC explains what altitude a pilot should expect at a certain fix (a navigation waypoint – see 'fix') or 'time'. In the event of an issue with communication, this assists the pilot to know that they are on course with the flight plan.
- **Expect Further Clearance (Time):** ATC usually will get back to the aviator at that time with instruction on clearance for the next maneuver.
- **Expect Further Clearance Via (Airways, Routes, or Fixes):** ATC will provide clearance on a maneuver but at a specific fix, route, or airway.

- **Expedite**: This is also an ATC instruction which normally advises the pilot on the best rate of climb or descent. It does not involve dramatic change. In most cases, it refers to a climb or descent, but is not limited to these.
- **FAA**: The Federal Aviation Administration is known as the FAA.
- **FARs** (Federal Aviation Regulations).
- **FBO** (Fixed-Base Operator): These are the operations where services are provided to aircraft such as refueling.
- **Firewall**: If you think of a house, the firewall is a wall that separates two amends or semi-detached houses so that in case a fire happens, the fire does not spread to the other amend or semi-detached house. This is the same with an aircraft. A firewall separates an engine from the other .s of the plane so that fire does not spread.
- **Five by five:** This term is used to indicate that broadcasts are clear and loud enough to be understood.
- **Flare:** A flare refers to an aircraft maneuver that takes place before a landing. The nose of the aircraft will point upwards which allows a descent to be completed.
- **Flight Level:** This refers to a level of constant atmospheric pressure which measures 29.92 inches in Mercury. Using an altimeter, a pilot would be able to measure the atmospheric pressure, usually in feet.
- **Flight Plan:** This is the plotted journey drafted before the flight begins. For a flight plan, the pilot needs to use a sectional chart to navigate the flight, considering terrain conditions. The pilot also calculates weather conditions and takes into account airspace regulations.
- **FRC (Request for Full Route Clearance):** Pilot/controller glossary explains that FRC or a Request for Full Route Clearance is when a pilot applies for an exact flight plan to be cleared by ATC. FRC should be made to also include receiving an ATC clearance for the initial flight plan and also when a filed IFR flight plan has been altered by a pilot, airline, or operations before take-off.
- **George**: This is the name of the autopilot system.
- **Glass cockpit:** This refers to a plane with a pilot panel which is completely digital.
- **Go Ahead:** Send your message. This is only used for this purpose. ATC is only permitting the pilot to send their message.
- **Go Around:** ATC is telling the pilot to abandon their approach (for landing) and the pilot should await further instruction. The aviator should be aware that for VFR or IFR flight plans that 'go around' needs to overfly the landing strip and "enter the traffic pattern via the crosswind". For an

IFR flight plan, the pilot needs to execute the missed approach procedure and wait for further instruction from ATC.

- **Gross Weight:** The total mass of the plane, all the people on board, and the cargo. This is also known as Payload.
- **Ground Control:** Ground Control are the employees who work on the ground or runway that are responsible for safety in this area.
- **Ground Effect:** This is an important term to remember for your exam preparation. As the aircraft comes for a landing, the lift on the vessel increases while the drag decreases. This is known as the 'ground effect'.
- **Groundspeed:** Epic Flight Academy defines 'groundspeed' as, "The horizontal speed of an aircraft relative to the surface below."
- **Handoff:** When ATC provides another controller with radar information of an aircraft. This can occur when ATC transfers the aircraft to another controller which deals with that specific class of airspace or to provide information of a specific nature.
- **Handshake:** When the computer of a satellite first communicates with the computer on the aircraft this is known as a handshake. This refers to the contact between the two computers which is typically in the form of a 'greeting'.
- **Hangar:** A kind of garage for airplanes where they can park, be repaired, or be maintained.
- Have Numbers: The pilot informs ATC that they have received the runway, altimeter, and wind data. It only applies to these three details.
- **Heavy (aircraft):** An aircraft which has a maximum demure weight of 136 tons or more.
- **Homing**: In this instance, they have not adjusted or corrected for wind and they are maintaining a bearing of zero degrees.
- **How Do You Hear Me?** This deals circularly with the quality of the broadcast between the pilot and ATC.
- **Hyperventilation:** This is a condition which describes a state of over-breathing. It is common enough among pilots as they are generally in stressful situations where decision-making is key. This state of over-breathing can have serious consequences such as choking or gulping. Therefore, it is treated with serious regard in aviation.
- **Hypoxia:** This is a type of altitude sickness. As oxygen becomes thinner as the altitude increases, pilots have lower levels of oxygen. They begin to feel dizzy and ill.
- **Ident**: The pilot requests to turn on the transponder identification feature which allows the aircraft to be identified.

- **If No Transmission Received For (Time):** This is another message given by ATC in case radio signal is lost between the pilot and ATC. If communication is lost, further instruction is given by ATC.
- **IFR (Instrument Flight Rules):** Also refer to VFR. Instrument Flight Rules refer to the umbrella rules regulations for aviation operation or flying under instrument meteorological conditions. All aviators are required to follow these regulations and plan IFR flight plans for different weather conditions.
- **ILS (Instrument Landing System):** This pertains to landings with low visibility. A pilot will switch to an ILS in these conditions using a ground system that advises on how to conduct a landing in conditions of low visibility.
- **Immediately:** This is another obvious one. ATC requires compliance without any delay.
- **Increase speed to (speed):** ATC asks the pilot for a speed adjustment necessary to execute ocular maneuver.
- **Indicated Airspeed (IAS):** The speed of the airplane is shown on a dial of the airspeed indicator. It does not calculate outside conditions such as wind, etc.
- **Instrument Rating:** This is a somewhat misleading term. Each pilot receives a rating for the types of adverse or difficult conditions they can fly or operate in.
- **Knot:** This is the measurement used for an airplane's speed, about one nautical mile or 1.15 statute miles.
- **KTAS (Knots True Airspeed):** KTAS refers to the speed of the aircraft in relation to the air mass.
- **Lateral axis (pitch):** This is one of the three motions of an aircraft. The lateral axis is the forward-backward motion of an airplane.
- **Lift:** This is the upward aerodynamic force which allows the plane to lift and work against gravity.
- **Longitudinal axis (roll):** This is one of the three motions of an aircraft. The longitudinal axis is the side-to-side motion of an airplane.
- **Low Altitude Alert: Check Altitude Immediately:** This is an order that requires immediate compliance. This is a safety alert to check your altitude.
- **Mayday:** No one wants to hear this term. A pilot says it three times to indicate serious danger.
- **Maintain:** The pilot is instructed to continue with the current altitude.
- **Make Short Approach:** A pilot is informed by ATC that his position in the traffic pattern has been shortened and a final approach should be expected.

- **Missed Approach:** An approach (landing) is not able to be performed or completed. Following a Missed Approach a pilot must continue with the approach, preparing for a landing but must repeat the process once again and obtain clearance from ATC.
- **MTOW** (Maximum Take-off Weight)
- **Navaid:** This is an instrument or device in an airplane providing navigation assistance to a pilot. It also gives the pilot data on their position.
- **Negative**: Opposite to 'affirmative'. Clearance or permission is not given by ATC.
- **Negative Contact**: This can be used for one or two purposes. First, the pilot informs ATC that he or she was not able to make contact with them. Second, following a traffic report or step from ATC, the aviator informs ATC that they have not yet encountered said incident. Typically, this awaits further instruction on traffic from ATC.
- **No Gyro Approach:** A radar or vector is experiencing a malfunction which necessitates the ATC to provide more instructions such as 'turn right or left'.
- **Non-Convective SIGMET:** This is a specific weather advisory for severe weather forecasts. It deals with forecasts for certain types of weather such as volcanic ash, dust, or a sandstorm over an area of 3,000 miles. It also refers to severe icing or turbulence over an area of 3,000 miles.
- **NOTAMs (Notices to Airmen):** These are announcements or broadcasts from ATC making pilots aware of any urgent or unusual circumstances, which should be known as flights are conducted.
- **NTZ (No Transgression Zone):** Aircrafts or flights are not permitted in the NTZ. The NTZ is a 2,000-foot-wide area which is situated parallel to the runway or SOIA.
- **Numerous Target Vicinity (location):** This is another instance which would relate to Heathrow. If there are too many targets on the radar, ATC uses this term to signal this situation to pilots.
- **OAT (Outside Air Temperature)**
- **Obstruction Clearance (Minimum Altitude):** When you go through sectional charts, you will use the charts to plan your trip to avoid obstructions. ATC will also provide instructions on the minimum altitude for avoiding such obstructions like water towers, etc. You will also need to get the clearance for this.
- **Off Course:** The aircraft is in a position fix on the radar which has **not been granted by ATC for that trip.**
- **Oil Pressure Gauge:** This is an instrument measuring lubricated engine oil inside the airplane engine.

- **On Course:** There are two uses for this term. Either ATC is informing a pilot that they are lined up for the final approach on their radar. Or it can be used to indicate that an aircraft is on the route centerline.
- **Out:** This signals the end of communication and no further conversation is expected.
- **Over:** This is another one familiar one. Unlike 'out' it means a transmission has ended, but further communication is expected.
- **Pan Pan:** Pan pan is used to signal that someone on a plane or a ship is an urgent situation. It is not to indicate that the individual's life is in danger, but there is some distress or urgency.
- **PIC (Pilot in Command):** With solo flights, there is only one pilot. However, with commercial or chartered flights, there can be more than one aviator on board. The PIC is the pilot who makes the decisions on which maneuvers to execute. In this case, the co-pilot will aid but will not be responsible for decision-making.
- **Pilot's Discretion:** ATC informs a pilot that he or she may begin a climb or descent when they deem such maneuvers to be advisable. This term is limited to these maneuvers.
- **Pitch (lateral axis):** This is the motion of the aircraft on the lateral axis, which from one to another side of the plane generally where the wings are located. The pitch works along with 'roll' and 'yaw'. See 'roll' and 'yaw'.
- **Preignition**: This is the ignition that happens in an internal combustion engine prior to ignition.
- **PFD (Primary Flight Display):** This one's acronym can be easily remembered. The PFD is the screen display that indicates the altitude, vertical speed, rate of turn, and horizon.
- **POH** (Pilot's Operating Handbook): A manual for pilots which provides key information on flight, aircraft operation, and safety regulations.
- **Quadra plane:** This is a plane with four wings.
- **Radar Contact:** ATC tells a pilot that the aircraft is a target within the ATC radar or surveillance.
- **Radar Contact Lost**: This term is used to signal the opposite of 'radar contact'. ATC radar or surveillance has been lost and ATC is not able to pick up data on the aircraft's position.
- **Radar Service Terminated:** ATC informs a pilot that their aircraft will not be monitored by radar any further and no radar services will be made by ATC for this aircraft. This can happen in a number of instances such as completion of an approach or when the pilot cancels a flight plan.
- **RAPCON** (Radar Approach Control Facility): Smith-Kohl's gives a succinct definition of this term:

- **Readback**: This is a request to 'read back my message to me'.
- **Reduce Speed to (Speed):** This is an instruction from ATC to make a decrease in speed.
- **Report**: This term is used to indicate a relay of information.
- **Request Full Route Clearance**: See FRC (Full Route Clearance).
- **Resume Normal Speed:** ATC indicates to the pilot that they can proceed with the normal operating speed.
- **Resume Own Navigation:** The pilot is signaled to proceed with responsibility for their own navigation.
- **Roger**: Contrary to popular belief, 'roger' does not mean 'yes', but it is an acknowledgement. This does not mean the pilot will comply with orders. See Affirmative, Negative, and Wilco.
- **Roll (Longitudinal axis):** The roll is the up and down motion of the plane, working with the ailerons to provide this rolling motion. The other motions which work with the plane are the 'yaw' and 'pitch'. Refer to these to understand the combination of the three motions.
- **RWY** (Runway): A section on aerodrome, rectangular in shape, which is demarcated for take-offs and landings.
- **Runway Heading**: This refers to the extended centerline of a demure runway and not the painted asphalt. When the direction is given, pilots are required to fly in accordance with the heading that agrees or meets the extended centerline of the demure runway.
- **Say Again**: Repeat information or an instruction.
- **Say Altitude**: A request from ATC for the current altitude.
- **Say Heading**: ATC requests the specific heading of the aircraft.
- **Short field**: This refers to a type of runway which is shorter in length which necessitates specific procedures to make a landing or take-off.
- **Soft field:** This is a type of runway that is unpaved and can be composed of grass or soil.
- **SIGMET** (Significant Meteorological Information): This is an advisory which relates to severe types of weather. This is a report given to the pilot about the weather which may affect the journey. There are two types, convective and non-convective. Convective includes dust and volcanic ash while non-convective regards powerful winds, turbulence, and thunderstorms. Compare with AIRMET.
- **SQUAWK:** Turn on specific modes or functions on the airplane transponder. This refers to a four-unit number which ATC uses to begin transmission with an aircraft.

- **Stall**: This causes a lot of fear for aspiring pilots on their exams. It is when the angle of attack is higher than the maximum lift, and the plane begins to lose altitude.
- **Standby**: When the pilot or ATC must wait for some time so that the pilot or ATC can deal with a responsibility of more urgency.
- **Stop Altitude SQUAWK:** ATC indicates that a pilot needs to turn off the automatic altitude reporting feature of the aircraft transponder.
- **Stop Stream:** ATC instructs a pilot to end all electronic activity.
- **Stop SQUAWK:** Turn off specific modes or functions on the airplane transponder.
- **Taxi**: When the aircraft is on the runway but is moving on the ground this is called 'taxiing'.
- **Terrain Clearance (Minimum Altitude):** Similarly, with obstruction clearance, you will also need a terrain clearance – maintaining a specific altitude – to safely manage a flight through a certain terrain. The airspace is affected by the terrain so you will also need clearance from ATC. This is what is meant by Terrain Clearance (Minimum Altitude).
- **That Is Correct**: What you understand is correct.
- **Torque**: A force which provides rotation.
- **Thrust**: Thrust is the power of the aircraft like when it travels through aerospace or down a runway.
- **Traffic**: There are two uses for this term. It can refer to numerous planes or it can indicate the transferal of an aircraft to another ATC (controller) to aid a separate maneuver.
- **Traffic in Sight**: The pilot informs ATC that traffic previously referred to can be seen.
- **Transponder:** A transponder is a device or instrument on aircraft which creates a code allowing the aircraft to be recognized on an ATC radar.
- **Unable**: The Pilot does not have the ability to follow ATC's instruction.
- **Uncontrolled Airspace**: You can also cross reference Airspace and Controlled Airspace. This is an area or class of airspace where ATC does not provide instructions. Nevertheless, airspace rules and VFR continue to apply.
- **Verify**: This is a request for the controller or pilot's confirmation of information.
- **Verify Specific Direction of Takeoff** (or Turns After Takeoff): ATC seeks to know which direction an aircraft plans to use for a demure.
- **Vertical Axis (yaw):** This is one of the three motions of an aircraft. The vertical axis is the upward-downward motion of an airplane.

- **VFR** (Visual Flight Rules): When the conditions allow a pilot to rely on vision, this is called Visual Flight Rules. It means that visibility is high. If a pilot would follow VFR, they would need to comply with the rules of VFR and they would first need clearance from ATC to follow VFR. Compare with IFR.
- **When Able**: This indicates that a pilot will comply with instructions given by ATC but at a later time.
- **Wilco:** Will Comply. The pilot has received ATC's instruction and will act accordingly.
- **Words Twice**: There is some trouble with communication, please repeat everything a second time.
- **Yaw (Vertical Axis)**: The Yaw is the rotation or motion that works along the vertical axis of the plane, typically, where the rudder is located. It acts in combination with the pitch and roll. See 'Pitch' and 'Roll'.
- **Zulu Time**: This is similar to Greenwich Mean Time. It is the universal time zone which allows all aviators to work with a standardized time zone.
- **Empennage**: This is a section of the tail which helps to stabilize the flight.
- **Fuselage**: The Fuselage is the main aircraft .. It is the mid-section or central portion where the passengers and cabin crew sit and where cargo is stored.
- **Horizontal stabilizer:** This is a small section of the tail which lifts providing further stability. It is also known as the tail plane.
- **Landing gear**: When an aircraft is on the ground, underneath the vehicle there is a . which supports its movements on the ground like taxiing. Read about 'taxiing' in the above section.
- **Master Switch:** This is the switch that is responsible for all the electric circuits in an airplane.
- **Propeller:** These are the blades which rotate at the nose of the aircraft. They initiate a rotational power into a linear thrust.
- **Rudder:** This is another section of the tail. It is a vertical surface that aids the side-to-side stability of an aircraft.
- **Tail:** The last section of the plane which assists with aerodynamics and stability.
- **Throttle:** This is a valve which regulates the amount of fuel that is allowed into the engine.
- **Yoke:** This is comparable to a car steering-wheel.

From the above section, it is clear that aviation terminology is specific. In fact, it is overly specific. Nevertheless, there are a number of similar terms that can aid your being able to grasp some of the language more easily such as 'unable' and 'when able' and 'affirmative' and 'negative'. Having said that, there are various acronyms to remember such as SIGMET and PFD.

This section has tried to provide you with some of the most commonly used and updated expressions that can assist you with the FAA knowledge, oral, and check ride.

Abbreviations on the cockpit instruments

This section will look at abbreviations on the cockpit instruments and their various displayed information. So to all aspiring flight students out there, go through these abbreviations since they will accompany you through your whole career as a Pilot.

- ADF - Automatic Direction Finder
- AIRS - Air data inertial reference system
- AFS - Auto Flight system
- AH/AI - Alpha Hotel or Alpha India
- AH/ AI - Artificial horizon or Altitude indicator
- ALT (Alpha Lima Tango) - Altimeter
- A/ THR (alpha /tango Hotel) - Auto Throttle
- B/A (Bravo/ Alpha) - Bank Angle
- CDI - Course Deviation Indicator
- CDU - Control Display Unit
- CKPT (Charlie kilo Papa tango) - Cockpit
- DG (Delta goal) - Directional Gyro (Heading Indicator)
- ECAM- Electronic Centralized Aircraft Monitor
- EFIS - Electronic Flight Instrument System
- EGT - Exhaust Gas Temperature
- EICAS - Engine Indication & Crew Alerting System,
- ENG - Engine
- F.D. - Flight Directors
- FMC - Flight Management Computer
- FMS - Flight Management System
- GPS - Global Positioning System
- GPWS - Ground Proximity Warning System
- G.S. - Ground speed
- HDG (hotel Delta Golf) - Heading
- HUD - Head up Display
- IAS - Indicated Airspeed
- LNAV - Lateral Navigation
- MCDU - Multi-Purpose Control Display Unit

- N1 - Low-pressure spool speed
- N2 - High-pressure spool speed
- NAV - Navigation
- BKN- Broken
- OVC- Overcast
- S.H. - Shower
- B.R. - Mist
- R.A. - Rain
- ND - Navigation display
- OBS - Omni bearing selector
- PFD - Primary flight display
- QNH - Altimeter setting/pressure reference
- MSL - Mean sea level
- RMI - Radi0 magnetic indicator
- SPD (Sierra papa Delta) - Speed
- STD (Sierra tango Delta) - Standard
- TAS - True Air Speed
- TCAS - Traffic Alerting Collision & Avoidance System
- THR (Tango Hotel Romeo) - Thrust/throttle
- TO/GA - Take-off/Go-around
- VHF - Very high frequency
- VNAV - Vertical navigation
- V/S - Vertical speed
- WXR - Weather radar

Radio Communication

You need to learn this radio communication alphabet skill and have them at the tip of your finger.

•	ALFA	•	INDIA
•	BRAVO	•	JULIETT
•	CHARLIE	•	KILO
•	DELTA	•	LIMA
•	ECHO	•	NOVEMBER
•	FOXTROT	•	OSCAR
•	GOLF	•	PAPA
•	HOTEL	•	QUEBEC

- ROMEO
- SIERRA
- TANGO
- UNIFORM
- VICTOR

- WHISKEY
- X-RAY
- YANKEE
- ZULU

For Numbers

- 0 - ZE- RO
- WUN
- TOO
- TREE
- FOW er
- FIFE
- SIX
- SEV en
- AIT
- NIN er
- Hundred - HUN dred
- Thousand - TOU SAND
- 500 - five hundred
- 4,500- four thousand five hundred
- 10,000 - one zero thousand
- 13,500 - one three thousand five hundred
- V12 - victor twelve
- J533 - Juliette Five Thirty-Three
- 10 - one zero
- 122.1 - one two two point one
- 12,000 - one two thousand
- 12,500 - one two thousand five hundred

- 190 - Flight level one Niner Zero
- 275 - Flight level two Seven Five
- (Magnetic course) 005 - zero zero five
- (Wind direction) 220 - wind two two zero
- (Speed) 250 - two five zero knots
- (speed) 190 - one niner zero knots
- Wilco = I will comply
- Roger = received and understood
- Affirmative = Yes
- Negative = No

REGULATIONS AND REQUIRED ACTIONS FOR PRIVATE PILOTS

REQUIRED INSTRUMENTS FOR FLIGHT DAY

- **T** – Tachometer for each engine (RPMs).
- – Oil pressure gauge.
- **F** – A fuel gauge showing the amount of fuel in each tank.
- **F*** – Floatation devices if operating outside of gliding distance from shore*.
- **A** – Anti-collision light system (i.e., a blinking red or white light).
- **A** – Airspeed indicator.
- **M** – Magnetic compass.
- **E** – Emergency locator transmitter (ELT).
- **S** – Safety belts.

These 4 items typically don't apply to training aircraft/flights. The manifold pressure gauge only applies to engines that have a turbocharger. Floatation devices apply to "for hire" operations over water. Most airplane engines are air cooled (not liquid cooled). Most training airplanes have fixed landing gear (not retractable gear). If flaming fruit isn't your thing, then maybe you can try out animals. Another popular mnemonic for required instruments during the day is "A GOOSE A CAT." This mnemonic does not include the items with an asterisk above.

- **A** – Anti-collision light system.
- **G** – Gauges; fuel gauge indicating the quantity of fuel in each tank.
- – Oil pressure gauge.
- – Oil temperature gauge.
- **S** – Safety belts.
- **E** – Emergency locator transmitter (ELT).
- **A** – Airspeed indicator.
- **C** – Compass.
- **A** – Altimeter.
- **T** – Tachometer.

NIGHT

"FLAPS"

- **F** – Fuses with spares (or Circuit Breakers, as with most aircraft).
- **L** – Landing light (if the aircraft is operated for hire).
- **A** – Anti-collision light system (a beacon or strobe lights).
- **P** – Position Lights (AKA "Nav. Lights").
- **S** – Source of electricity adequate for all installed electrical equipment (e.g., an alternator).

NOTE: In addition to those instruments required by the Federal Aviation Regulations, there may be items that the manufacturer requires in order to maintain the aircraft's airworthiness. So, to correctly list the required instrumentation, you should also look in the POH (usually section 6 - Weight and Balance) to see if your airplane has a required "equipment list" of items that may not directly be listed in "TOMATO

FLAAMES" and "FLAPS." Example: airplane manufacturers will typically require the stall warning horn and other specific gauges.

MODE C TRANSPONDER

A mode C transponder (i.e., an altitude-encoding transponder) is required in the following areas:

• In or above class C airspace.

• At and above 10,000' MSL.

MINIMUM EQUIPMENT LIST

• A Minimum Equipment List (MEL) is a definite list of instruments, equipment, and set of procedures that allows an individual aircraft to be operated under specific conditions with malfunctioning equipment.

o Most GA airplanes **do not** operate with an MEL (FAR 91.213), rather, they operate with "TOMATO FLAMES" or "A GOOSE A CAT" (FAR 91.205).

• An MEL must be FAA-approved and is specific to a particular make and model aircraft.

• All airlines operate with MELs in order to reduce cancellations and delays.

• An airplane operator may choose to operate with an MEL in order to reduce 'down time' of an airplane when encountering maintenance issues.

o *EXAMPLE: Normally, it is prohibited to fly with an inoperative fuel gauge.*

However, with an MEL, it may be possible to operate without one working fuel gauge so long as the pilot-in-command (PIC) operates under certain guidelines and procedures, such as dipping the fuel tanks to measure fuel, requiring 2 hours of reserve fuel, etc.

INOPERATIVE EQUIPMENT – If a pilot determines that there is inoperative equipment on board—one that is not required by the manufacturer, regulations, or Airworthiness Directives (ADs)—then the pilot must remove and/or deactivate the inoperative item and placard it as "INOPERATIVE."

AUTOMATIC DEPENDENT SURVEILLANCE BROADCAST (ADS-B)

ADS-B is a system that enhances safety by broadcasting an aircraft's GPS

location approximately once every second. The broadcast improves ATC

efficiency and the ability to maintain aircraft separation, especially in areas that would normally not have adequate radar coverage. ADS-B will eventually replace traditional radar as the primary source for ATC.

• **ADS-B Out:** An onboard system that automatically broadcast the aircraft tail number, GPS location, and altitude to ground base stations (for ATC) or directly to other pilots (those with ADS-B In). ADS-B Out units are usually integrated in GPS units, transponders, or beacon lights.

• **ADS-B In**: An onboard system that receives the location and altitude of surrounding aircraft, as well as other beneficial features, such as updated weather reports (e.g., METARs, radar images, etc.) and TFRs. ADS-B In units enhances a pilot's overall situational awareness (SA).

ADS-B Out (*installed* in the aircraft) is required in the following areas:

- Class A-B-C airspace.
- Class E airspace, at or above 10,000' MSL (except below 2,500' AGL).
- Within 30NM of Class B airspace (mode C veil).
- Above the lateral limits of Class B and C airspace, up to 10,000' MSL.
- Class E airspace over the Gulf of Mexico—above 3,000' MSL and within 12 NM of the coast.

AIRCRAFT MAINTENANCE & RECORDS

INSPECTIONS REQUIRED

- Annual Inspection every 12 calendar months.

- 100 Hour Inspection every 100 hours of tachometer/engine time.
- Transponder (altitude-encoding/"mode C") check every 24 calendar months (if flying in an area where a mode C transponder is required).
- Emergency Locater Transmitter (ELT) every 12 calendar months.
- The ELT battery must be replaced when it has been used for 1 cumulative hour *or* when half of the battery's shelf life has expired.
- Pilots may test ELTs (on 121.5) during the first 5 minutes of every hour.
- Compliance with all Airworthiness Directives (ADs).
- All inspection records must be logged in the aircraft maintenance logs.

Try using "AVIATES" (though some of the inspections are only for IFR).

- **A** – Annual inspection (12 calendar months).
- **V** – VOR check (**IFR only** – within the last 30 days).
- **1** – 100-hour inspection (for hire only; not required if you own the airplane).
- **A** – Airworthy Directives (compliance with all ADs as required).
- **T** – Transponder inspection (24 calendar months).
- **E** – ELT inspection (12 calendar months).
- **S** – Static system ("pitot-static") inspection (**IFR only** - 24 calendar months).

CFI TIP: Pilots should know where to locate the logbook entries for these inspections, as well as the ADS-B installation (since ADS-B requirements are relatively new).

AIRWORTHINESS DIRECTIVES (AD)

- An Airworthiness Directive (AD) is a notification to owners of certified aircraft that a known safety deficiency must be corrected.
- ADs may address the replacement, testing, or inspection of any part within the aircraft (e.g., within the airframe, engine, propeller, landing gear, etc.).
- All ADs must be complied with in order to maintain airworthiness; an aircraft with an AD that has not been complied with is not airworthy.
- ADs may be divided into two categories (one-time & recurring): o Those that need emergency attention and should be complied with before any further flight (e.g., must replace a certain bad fuel line immediately).
- Those that require compliance within a specified time (i.e., a certain tachometer time, by a certain date, etc.).
- Some ADs are repetitive and require continued compliance every so often (e.g., every annual inspection, ever 500 hours of tach. time, etc.).

AIRFRAME & POWERPLANT (A&P) MECHANICS

- A&P mechanics are the only people authorized to work on aircraft (*beyond* preventive maintenance).
- A&P mechanics complete the majority of maintenance and alterations on aircraft, such as completing a 100-hour or replacing an alternator.
- An inspection annually **must** be signed for by an A&P with Inspection Authorization (A&P IA), which is a higher-level A&P mechanic.
- Some maintenance requires specific certification: Avionic Technicians for radios, GPS units, etc.; Certificated Repair Stations for flight instruments.

PREVENTIVE MAINTENANCE

- Preventive maintenance includes simple/minor preservation maintenance, such as the replacement of small parts not involving complex assembly operations (i.e., not requiring an A&P mechanic).
- Private Pilots are allowed to perform preventive maintenance.
- Examples of preventive maintenance includes items such as: replenishing hydraulic fluid, changing the oil, or inflating the tires.
- Pilots who perform preventive maintenance must make an aircraft logbook entry with the type of maintenance, the tachometer reading, the date, and the pilot's information (name, certificate number, and signature).

REQUIRED DOCUMENTS FOR AIRCRAFT

"AROW-G" The following documents must be on board prior to each flight: **A** – Airworthiness Certificate.

R – Registration Certificate (*NOTE: expires every 3 years*).

O – Operating limitations (e.g., POH).

W – Weight and Balance (usually located in the POH).

G – GPS Supplement (sometimes required, per the airplane's equipment list, for airplanes equipped with certain on-board GPS units).

PILOT REGULATIONS

PRIVATE PILOT PRIVILEGES AND LIMITATIONS

- You may operate as a pilot in command (PIC) of an aircraft that is carrying passengers but may not be compensated for it.
- May not pay less than the "pro-rata share" of the operating expenses.

EXAMPLE 1: A flight with a pilot + 3 passengers = everyone can pay 25%.

EXAMPLE 2: If only the pilot and one passenger pay (*regardless of total number passengers*) = pilot must pay at least 50%.

- This includes fuel, oil, parking fees, and other operational costs.
- May act as PIC of an aircraft used in a passenger-carrying airlift sponsored by a charity or non-profit organization (pilot must have at least 500 hours).
- May act as PIC and be reimbursed for aircraft operating expenses that are directly related to search and location operations.

REQUIRED DOCUMENTS FOR PILOTS

Pilots must have the following in their possession during each flight:

- A valid pilot certificate.
- A valid medical certificate (*or a U.S. Driver's License with BasicMed*).
- A valid government-issued photo ID.

MEDICAL CERTIFICATE

A Private Pilot must hold at least a 3rd Class FAA medical certificate. It is required to be in the pilot's possession at all times when acting as a pilot.

Alternatively, a Private Pilot *may* operate certain aircraft with a Basic Med.

There are currently three classes of FAA medical certificates.

BASICMED

Basic Med allows private pilots to operate certain aircraft with only their U.S. driver's license (i.e., an FAA medical is not required).

To qualify for a Basic Med, pilots must:

- Have a valid U.S. Driver's License.

- Have had a medical certificate that was valid after July 14, 2006.
- NOT have had the most recent FAA medical certificate denied, revoked, or suspended.
- NOT have a medical condition that requires a "Special Issuance" (61.89).
- Undertake a physical examination (with your primary doctor) every 4 years.
- Complete an approved online course every 2 years (e.g., with AOPA).

There are limitations with the aircraft that a pilot can fly with a Basic Med: o Maximum of a 6-seat airplane (maximum of 5 passengers).

- The MTOW of the airplane cannot exceed 6,000 lbs.
- Flights are limited to the U.S., U.S. territories, and The Bahamas.
- Must fly below FL180 and at maximum speed of 250 KIAS.
- Cannot fly for compensation or hire.

FLIGHT REVIEW

• A practical test that leads to a *new* certificate or rating (e.g., an instrument rating checkride) may be substituted for a flight review.

• Successful completion of a flight review will include: o A minimum of **1 hour of flight** and **1 hour of ground** training from a CFI.

A signed endorsement from the CFI

• Essentially, a flight review is very similar to a mini checkride.

CURRENCY REQUIREMENTS

Pilots must have a flight review within the preceding 24 calendar months.

If a pilot wishes to carry passengers, they must have, within the preceding 90 days:

- 3 takeoffs and 3 landings (may be touch-and-goes) if flying with passengers during daylight.
- 3 takeoffs and 3 full-stop landings between 1 hour after sunset until 1 hour before sunrise, in order to fly passengers at night.
- Landings at night count for the daylight currency, but not vice-versa.
- Must be in same category and class (and type, if a type rating is required).

NOTE: Pilots should also consider maintaining "proficiency." Since "currency" only pertains to meeting the prescribed FAA minimums, "proficiency" requires a pilot to maintain personal minimums and continuously practice one's skills to obtain a high level of safety. The FAA developed the WINGS program to help pilots continually sharpen their skills. For more information visit: www.FAASafety.gov. Furthermore, the WINGS program can help pilots to complete portions of a flight review.

CHANGE OF ADDRESS

A holder of a pilot certificate, who has had a change in permanent address, must notify the FAA within 30 days of that change.

Notification can be made by mail or online at: www.FAA.gov.

ALCOHOL

Within 8 hours after consuming alcohol ("8 hours - bottle to throttle").

While having a blood alcohol content (BAC) of 0.04 or greater. Except in an emergency, no pilot of an aircraft may allow a person who appears to be under the influence of drugs or poison to be transported aboard that aircraft.

UNDERSTANDING "CATEGORY" VS. "CLASS"

• "Category" is used to determine the different category of aircraft (e.g., airplane, rotorcraft, glider, hot-air balloon, etc.).

• "Class" breaks down each category to a further level. For airplanes, class is broken down to the following 4 classes: single engine land or sea and multi-engine land or sea (**ASEL, ASES, AMEL, AMES**).

COMPLEX AIRPLANE

An airplane that has retractable landing gear, controllable pitch propeller, and wing flaps. In order to fly a complex airplane, a pilot must: receive flight and ground training from a CFI or receive a one-time endorsement from the CFI.

HIGH-PERFORMANCE AIRPLANE

• An airplane that has an engine with *more* than 200 horsepower.

• In order to fly a high-performance airplane, a pilot must: receive flight and ground training from a CFI or receive a one-time endorsement from the CFI.

TAILWHEEL (AKA "TAIL DRAGGER")

• An airplane with 2 main wheels in the front and 1 tailwheel in the back.

HIGH ALTITUDE/PRESSURIZED AIRCRAFT

An airplane with a pressurized cabin that can fly *above* FL250.

In order to fly a pressurized airplane that can fly above FL250, a pilot must:

- Receive flight and ground training from a CFI.
  - Receive a one-time endorsement from the CFI.

TYPE RATING

A type rating is required for any pilot wishing to fly an airplane that has an MTOW of *more* than 12,500 lbs. *and/or* is powered by turbojets. In other words, it is a "rating" to fly a specific type of aircraft (e.g., King Air 350, Cessna Citation X, Gulfstream V, Boeing 737, Airbus A320, etc.).

A pilot must go through ground training that includes a thorough understanding of all of the systems of the airplane, as well as successfully passing a checkride in an airplane or a simulator.

FUEL REQUIREMENTS

Pilots must be able to fly to the destination and have enough reserve fuel to fly at a normal cruise speed for:

- 30 minutes if flying during the day.
- 45 minutes if flying at night.

CFI TIP: For safety, pilots should always plan on having at least 1 hour of reserve fuel.

SAFETY BELTS AND SHOULDER HARNESS REQUIREMENTS

*For crew members (in this case, **pilots**):*

- Safety belts and shoulder harness must be worn for takeoff, taxi, and landing.
- Only the shoulder harness *may* be removed during cruise flight.

For passengers:

- Safety belts and shoulder harness must be worn for takeoff, taxi, and landing.
- Shoulder harness *and* safety belt may be removed during cruise flight.

AIRSPEED RESTRICTIONS

• Below 10,000' MSL: 250 KIAS.

• At or below 2,500' AGL and within 4NM of Class C or D: 200 KIAS.

• Airspace under Class B or in a Class B Corridor: 200 KIAS.

SUPPLEMENTAL OXYGEN REQUIREMENTS

Supplemental oxygen must be used by pilots and supplied to passengers should the cabin pressure reach high altitudes (see table below). Only aviation-grade oxygen should be used.

ALTITUDES REGULATIONS

The minimum required flight crew (i.e., **the pilot**) **12,501 – 14,000 must use** supplemental oxygen **after 30 minutes** within these altitudes. The minimum required flight crew (i.e., **the pilot**) **14,001** – Above must use supplemental oxygen **at all times** for the duration of flight at those altitudes. Each occupant (i.e., **passengers**) must be **provided 15,001 – Above** with supplemental oxygen.

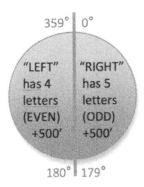

VFR CRUISING ALTITUDES

The following should be applied when flying below FL180 and above 3,000' AGL:

- Magnetic course of 0°-179°:
- Odd thousands + 500 feet (e.g., 7,500, etc.).
- Magnetic course of 180°-359°:

Even thousands + 500 feet (e.g., 6,500, etc.).

NOTE: Altitudes without +500' (e.g., 7,000', 8,000', etc.) are reserved for IFR flights.

MINIMUM SAFE ALTITUDE TERM MEANING/REQUIREMENTS

An altitude allowing— *if power should fail*— an emergency landing without **"MINIMUM SAFE ALTITUDE"** undue hazard to people or property on the surface.

Minimum of 1,000 feet over the highest obstacle with a horizontal distance of **"CONGESTED AREAS"** 2,00' feet.

The FAR/AIM does not define "congested area."

"OTHER THAN CONGESTED Minimum of 500 feet above the **AREAS"** surface.

"OVER OPEN WATER OR Minimum of 500 feet from the nearest **SPARSELY POPULATED AREAS"** person, vessel, vehicle, or structure.

CFI TIP: Pilots should also consider using a higher altitude and/or possibly a different route (along highways and flat land) when operating on a x-country flight at night.

SPECIAL VFR (SVFR)

Requirements:

Visibility 1 SM and remain clear of clouds.

 Can be used in the controlled airspace of an airport (Class B, C, D, and E).

 Must be requested by the pilot with ATC. In order to request SVFR at night (sunset to sunrise): o Pilot must be IFR certified o Aircraft must be IFR equipped.

CFI TIP: SVFR is a great tool, but it should be reserved for pilots with lots of experience. New pilots should be cautious about exercising SVFR requests.

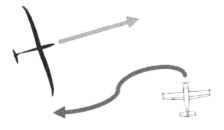

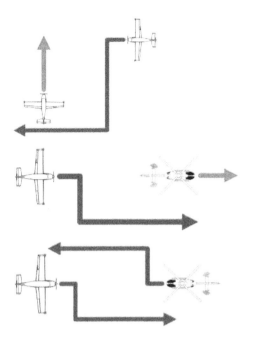

RIGHT OF WAY RULES: CONVERGING*

The right of way rules for converging aircraft differ than with aircraft that are head-on or being overtaken. In a converging situation, the right of way rules depends if the aircraft are of the same category or not.

SAME CATEGORY - When aircraft of the *same* category (e.g., airplane and airplane) are converging, the **priority** is given to the aircraft on **the right.**

DIFFERENT CATEGORY - When aircraft of *different* categories are converging, the aircraft that is least maneuverable has the priority.

"Big R" (BG AAR)

B – Balloons.

G – Glider (as shown).

A – Airship.

A – Air refueling or banner towing aircraft.

R – Rotorcraft or Airplane (as shown).

*NOTE 1: Aircraft with a **GREEN** *arrow have the right of way, and aircraft with a* **RED** *arrow must maneuver to avoid a collision.*

*NOTE 2: An aircraft in distress ALWAYS has the right-of-way over

ALL *other aircraft.*

*NOTE 3: When landing, the aircraft that is lower has the right of way.

RIGHT OF WAY RULE: HEAD-ON & OVERTAKING*

In a head-on or overtaking situation, it does *not* matter if aircraft are the same category or not.

HEAD-ON – In this case, neither has the right of away and both aircraft must alter course to the **right**.

OVERTAKING – **An** aircraft overtaking another aircraft must alter course to the **right**. The airplane that is being overtaken has the right of way.

Q&A

Part 1

1. What is airspeed velocity?

The airspeed at which an aircraft moves through the air.

If so, you might want to take this short private pilot exam! This is not a test of knowledge, but rather of understanding. If you understand basic concepts, then it's likely that you will understand better than someone else who is not as familiar with them even if they know more about them. Answer the questions below and find out how well you do on understanding what needs to happen in order for an airplane to fly!

2. How does flight occur?

When a wing travels faster than its critical speed it generates enough lift to support its weight.

3. How is lift created?

When the air flows across the upper surface at a faster speed than the lower surface, the airflow creates a pressure difference and air accelerates downward.

4. When is lift generated?

When an airplane is moving forward powered by its propeller, there exists a downward force due to pressure difference created by airflow over the top of the wing and underside of the propeller. When this force exceeds weight of aircraft, it creates lift which supports aircraft weight.

5. What is thrust produced?

Thrust can be produced if airplane's propeller/fan or wings generate enough pressure on air flowing through them which makes them capable of doing work on air.

6. What is angle of attack?

Angle of attack refers to angle of relative wind to the chord line (half of wing) in flight.

7. What is angle of incidence?

Angle which the chord line forms with horizontal plane or fuselage.

8. What does angle of attack make possible?

The ability for airfoil/wing to generate lift/downward force for its weight and support it in flight.

9. Where are wings located on an airplane?

They are usually located on the wingtips, but can also be mounted over, under, behind or in front of the main fuselage.

(1) Over: The wings are attached above the main fuselage.

(2) Under: The wings are attached in front of the main fuselage.

(3) Near: The wings are mounted near to the fuselage.

(4) Behind: The wings are mounted behind the main fuselage.

(5) In front of: The wings are located in front of the main fuselage.

10. What is aerodynamic efficiency?

The ratio of lift over drag force generated by an airfoil/wing moving through air in flight relative to its total weight, thrust or power input .

11. What is the difference between an airplane wing and a bird wing?

An airplane wing typically has an airfoil cross-section or airfoil section which is symmetric about the aircraft's center line, unlike the wings of a bird which are usually swept back and have an asymmetric airfoil section.

12. What is thrust force?

Thrust force refers to forward force exerted on the airplane by its propeller/fan powered by its engine(s). This can be produced if it has enough pressure on air flowing through it which makes it capable of doing work on air.

13. What is drag force?

Drag(force) refers to backward force exerted on the airplane by its wings and other external surfaces. Drag may occur due to high-pressure air flowing over the external surface of an airplane flowing backward relative to its direction of flight and thus creating a retarding force.

14. How does thrust force help produce lift?

If thrust exceeds aerodynamic drag on an airplane, thrust will produce a forward acceleration which lifts it into the air.

15. What are two categories of propulsion in terms of aircraft?

(1) Powered : Propulsion in which the engine is used to power aircraft forward (usually while fueled by an onboard fuel tank).

(2) Unpowered : Propulsion in which the engine is not used to power aircraft forward (usually can't be fueled like gas or liquid fuel-powered engines).

16. What are the two categories of propulsion in terms of aircraft?

(1) Fixed wing : Propeller/fan, wings and tail surfaces are used to produce thrust and lift to support weight in flight.

(2) Rotary wing : Tail rotor, rotor blades and a transmission are used to produce thrust and lift to support weight in flight.

17. What is power?

So, power refers to the rate at which work is done while an airplane is moving through the air. It refers to the amount of thrust available if thrust is needed over a given period of time. The unit of power is the horse power (hp), which defines the rate at which work is done when one player pulls on a rope that weighs 50 pounds and moves it upwards for 10 feet in one second.

If you want to do more work or lift heavier loads, you will need to increase your power output. If your power-output decreases, then your ability to carry out tasks or move loads will also decrease. If you double the rate at which you pull up on this 50-pound weight and pull it up two feet per second instead of one foot per second, then your power-output has increased by 4 times. [Assuming you do not get tired over a 10-second period.]

(1) Horsepower: British unit of power. 1 horsepower is equivalent to 746 watts. 1 hp = 550 ft-lb/min or 746 W.

(2) Watt: SI unit of power, one watt is equivalent to one joule per second. 1 W = 1J/s

18. What is thrust?

Thrust refers to the upward force produced by an airplane propeller/fan, wings or other components. It is measured in pounds (lbf) and is produced by the aerodynamic forces acting on the airplane due to its forward motion.

If an airliner needs a 9 lbs/sec of thrust to propel it up through air, then it will require 8.8 SCFM of fuel per second at cruising speed going forward with no wind drag. If a jet needs a 9 lbs/sec to travel at Mach 0.85 speed, then it will use 6 SCFM of fuel per second at cruise speed going forward with no wind drag.

19. How is drag related to thrust?

Drag results from the point at which the air flowing over an aircraft component flows faster than the speed of that component. This creates a drag force causing it backward in air, creating a retarding force. If it is not enough to counteract weight of airplane, then there is a loss of lift on airplane which results in aircraft falling and crashing.

(1) Drag force: Downward thrust created by airflow over an airplane's wing or tail surfaces which create a retarding force on aircraft relative to its weight in flight.

(2) Thrust force: Upward force created by airflow over an airplane's propeller/fan or other components which allow it to travel for a given time and distance

20. What are the four conditions that are necessary for flight?

1. Air must be moving forward through the wing or tail surface

2. There must be enough pressure on air at the wing or tail surface to provide lift

3. The air must be moving fast enough through the wing or tail surface

4. The wing or tail surface must have an appropriate shape

21. What are the two categories of aircraft?

(1) Fixed wing : Propeller/fan, wings and tail surfaces are used to produce thrust and lift to support weight in flight.

(2) Rotary wing : Tail rotor, rotor blades and a transmission are used to produce thrust and lift to support weight in flight.

Part 2

1. What is the formula for speed?

The formula for speed is: Velocity = Distance / Time. Velocity is the speed of an object moving through air (in metros per second). Distance is the distance traveled (in metros), where both must be expressed in SI units. Time is usually expressed in hours, minutes and seconds (or years, decades, centuries etc.) per SI unit.

2. When do I start my turn to enter the traffic pattern?

The decision to make a turn in frequency is made at the very beginning of the flight. The flight crew need to decide if they plan to make a downwind entry or an approach/runway entry (if they are proceeding directly into the traffic pattern). They also need to decide if they will make an initially base-to-final approach, or will initiate a climb/descent phase first in order for them to determine their final approach course and altitude (and therefore, their landing distance) with more accuracy.

3. When do I start my turn?

Air traffic control is responsible for providing service from unpowered aircraft (i.e. gliders) to powered aircraft, and therefore can decide not to provide separation from unpowered aircraft (gliders) if the traffic volume is high. A glider in this case would normally remain on its original course for a longer period of time until the air traffic controller feels it safe for them to turn. It is important for pilots of unpowered aircraft (gliders) to listen carefully to instructions given by air traffic control in order to remain clear of other aircraft movement.

4. What direction do I turn when entering the pattern?

When making a base-to-final approach, pilots make a right turn at the end of their downwind leg. The turn will put them on a base leg of an approach, which is a leg that is roughly 45 degrees from the runway centerline. When making this turn, it is important to keep the direction of the turn constant so that pilots do not need to increase or decrease their rpm as they make this turn (this may lead to a stall).

5. What direction do I enter the downwind?

When making an approach/runway entry, pilots initially fly on their base leg. Therefore, if they are flying inbound towards the airport, they will initially make a right hand turn in order to line up approximately 45 degrees from the runway centerline. The pilot then completes their base turn and starts the downwind leg of their approach. If pilots are flying inbound towards the airport and are planning to land at an Airport Freeway Intersection Approach, they will initially line up on the runway centerline (or parallel taxiway), make a right hand turn, then complete a 180 degree turn to match traffic pattern entry heading (the pilot often refers to this as a "Big Obvious Right Turn," or "BIORUT") from which they will begin their initial descent.

6. How do I enter my traffic pattern?

When making an initial vertical descent or an approach/runway entry, pilots initially fly on their base leg. Therefore, if they are flying inbound towards the airport, they will initially make a right hand turn in order to line up approximately 45 degrees from the runway centerline. The pilot then completes their base turn and starts the downwind leg of their approach. If pilots are flying inbound towards the airport and are planning to land at an Airport Freeway Intersection Approach, they will initially line up on the runway centerline (or parallel taxiway), make a right hand turn, then complete a 180 degree turn to match traffic pattern entry heading (the pilot often refers to this as a "Big Obvious Right Turn," or "BIORUT") from which they will begin their initial descent.

7. When must I turn?

Air traffic control is responsible for providing service from unpowered aircraft (i.e. gliders) to powered aircraft, and therefore can decide not to provide separation from unpowered aircraft (gliders) if the traffic volume is high. A glider in this case would normally remain on its original course for a longer period of time until the air traffic controller feels it's safe for them to turn. It is important for pilots of unpowered aircraft (gliders) to listen carefully to instructions given by air traffic control in order to remain clear of other aircraft movement.

8. How do I avoid colliding with another aircraft?

Managing the separation between your aircraft and another aircraft is a pilot's responsibility. It is their own responsibility to make sure they don't collide with another aircraft by maintaining a safe distance. If two articles are being separated by a distance of 1,000 feet or more and are on a crash course, they are said to have been "resolving the conflict". A pilot's first consideration when resolving conflict should be avoidance action (e.g. alter course). If this does not result in avoiding the other aircraft, then the pilot should initiate maneuvering (e.g. turn, climb, descent).

9. Am I cleared to land?

Once an approach has been completed, the first step is to start the landing process by going through the traffic pattern if a standard instrument approach has not been selected. The last check for air traffic control clearance is when a pilot calls "Cleared Approach," or "cleared for landing" and turns final for landing. When a pilot says "cleared to land," they mean that:

A pilot may call "Cleared to Land" even without receiving a response from air traffic control.

10. How do I know which runway is in use?

When making an approach to a runway, it is important for pilots to listen for the word "runway" when air traffic control announces the approach course. If a pilot is not given a runway number at this point, they should request it (e.g. "Hilo Tower ... I'm looking for the FOUR Left ... can you give me the three-letter identifier?").

11. What are visual reference points?

Visual reference points are those reference points that can be seen from the cockpit and will allow pilots to determine their position relative to other surfaces that are usually perpendicular to the flight path of an aircraft (e.g. airport perimeter fence, roadway, etc.).

12. What are non-visual reference points?

Non-visual reference points are those reference points that will allow a pilot to determine their position relative to other surfaces that are not usually perpendicular to the flight path of an aircraft (e.g. airport runway, centerline, touchdown zone lights). Non-visual reference points often rely on the pilot's GPS system for guidance (or visual contact with another aircraft in some cases).

13. How do I use non-visual reference points?

Non-visual reference points are used to find a particular location in relation to a runway. This is done by identifying the specific non-visual reference point and repeating it aloud until the pilot can see or hear that non-visual reference point. For example, if the pilot wants to hear whether they are left or right of the touchdown zone lights, they would repeat "touchdown zone lights" and wait for an indication that they are either right or left, as well as how far.

14. How do I tell if I'm high or low?

Pilots should listen carefully when receiving instructions from air traffic control with regard to their vertical positioning (i.e. "Low" or "High"). If a pilot receives a message saying "BEARING YAW 150 DEGREES, TURN RIGHT NOW," they need to make sure that they understand the meaning of the instructions (e.g. "I'm being told to turn right now.").

With regard to vertical positioning, pilots should always avoid flying in areas where natural obstacles (e.g. canyons) or man-made obstacles are present.

15. What is one purpose for using reciprocating engines?

A. better distribution of heat

B. to preserve cylinder head duration and maintain lower temperatures

C. They are relatively simple and inexpensive to operate

If you don't recognize some of these things we've talked about, you know it's probably not going to get the correct answer.

They're relatively simple and inexpensive, **which is C.**

By the way, most engines out there will typically cost 20 to 50 thousand dollars for replacement and sometimes more. The engines need to be overhauled somewhere between 1800 to 2000 hours, though manufacturers are slightly different. One of the purposes of reciprocating engines is that they're relatively simple. In that sense, they're also inexpensive to operate, at least on the day-to-day side of things.

16. One purpose of the dual ignition system on an aircraft engine is to provide for

A. improved engine performance

B. uniform heat distribution

C. balanced cylinder head pressure keep in

There are two seemingly correct answers for this question, but there's one better answer than another that the FAA wants.

The number one reason is because of improved engine performance. Now uniform heat distribution is correct. But as I said, with the FAA and most government tests, you take out the best answer rather than just the correct answer.

17. If an airplane weighs 4,500 pounds, what approximate weight would the airplane structure require to support during a 45° banked turn while maintaining altitude?

A. 4,500 pounds

B. 6,750 pounds

C. 7,200 pounds

I will show you both ways to do this. We're going to find 45° on the chart. Then you have a load factor n number which is 1.414. So all we are going to do is to use the first method to figure it out, which is

4500 pounds x 1.414

= 6,363 pounds

Now you're going to notice that this is not a potential answer, but the closest number we can come up with is the 6363. The nearest number we have will be 6750 pounds, and 4500 is too light while 7200 is too heavy.

The second way of coming up with this number is this. I can use the load factor chart and figure out where 45° is, and I will use a ruler to draw it reasonably straight. So down 40 and 45, I will draw a line kind of too far to the right. I'm going to take the intersects and draw them straight across. So what I'm coming up with is about 1.5 between 1 and the 2.

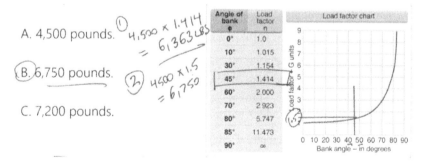

Angle of bank ϕ	Load factor n
0°	1.0
10°	1.015
30°	1.154
45°	1.414
60°	2.000
70°	2.923
80°	5.747
85°	11.473
90°	∞

What I can do with this number is take the same weight of the aircraft, 4500 pounds and multiply it by 1.5.

4500 pounds x 1.5

= 6750 pounds

In this case, if I'm using the chart, the second method will get me the exact number, which is B 6,750 pounds. Honestly, I think using the load factor the 1.414 is probably a more accurate number.

137

18. An electrical system failure (battery and alternator) occurs during flight. In this situation, you would:

A. experiencing avionics equipment failure

B. probably experienced failure of the engine ignition system, fuel gauges, aircraft lighting system, and avionics equipment

C. probably experienced engine failure due to the loss of the engine-driven fuel pump and also experienced failure of the radio equipment, lights, and all instruments that require alternating current.

Remember, the battery will provide about 20 to 30 minutes of power. Then the alternator is usually associated with the engine, so once you get the engine running, the alternator is recharging the battery in real-time, depending on whether it's an alternator or generator. If both systems went out, you would experience an avionics equipment failure. But when we look at this, the question is primarily to understand the magnetos with the engine. Is the engine going to quit when the battery and the alternator die? **In addition, the answer to that is No.**

So experiencing the avionics equipment failure is a **correct answer, which is A.**

19. The operating principle of floating carburetors is founded on:

A. automatically metering air over the venturi as the airplane gained altitude.

B. pressure difference of air at the venturi throat and at the air entry.

C. increases in air velocity in the throat of the venturi, causing an increase in air pressure.

Pushing the throttle forward too fast is not going to cause the engine to flood. But if you over prime the engine, that's probably the fastest way to start the engine to flood. It put too much fuel in there, which makes it completely flooded.

Just like I said in the last statement, it's the difference in air pressure at the venturi's throat and the air inlet. So that's the operating principle because it is based on a venturi. **The answer is B.**

20. Which condition is most favorable to the development of carburetor icing?

A. Any temperature below freezing and relative humidity of less than 50%

B. A temperature range of 32 to 50°F and low humidity levels

C. A Temperature range of 20 to 70°F and high humidity.

The answer to the question is C which is the temperature between 20 and 70°
higher humidity. There's more moisture content in the air.

Part 3

1. How do I avoid colliding with an aircraft?

Air traffic control will normally specify which type of aircraft a pilot should be
aware of when approaching an airport, for example: Large jets/bombers, general
aviation, helicopters/hangers etc... Pilots should be aware of all types of aircraft that
are operating in the area.

Air traffic control will also specify the distance that a pilot must maintain between
their aircraft and any other aircraft that is on final approach. If a pilot does not
understand the altitude restrictions, they should ask for clarification from the air
traffic controller with regard to their height clearance.

A good way to remember this would be to say: "Remember – Air Traffic Control
Says...9,000 feet and I'm going 9,000 feet" (or simply "9K"). Air traffic controllers
will always state how much separation is required between two aircraft before
receiving a "CLEARANCE" from pilots.

2. How do I avoid colliding with obstacles?

Obstacle avoidance is the ability to detect, avoid, and/or maneuver around natural
or man-made obstacles. If an aircraft approaches a canyon that air traffic control has
not specified, a pilot must be able to identify this canyon as an obstacle. Similarly,
if a pilot is instructed to descend below the altitude of another aircraft (i.e. "This
traffic is at 7K... descend to 6K"), they must identify the other aircraft as an obstacle.

A pilot should avoid flying in canyon areas by staying above an altitude of 1,250
feet. This will allow aircraft to be over land for an extra 500 feet. For example, a
pilot flying at 11K would be flying in an area where the canyon is 2,000 feet below
the plane. Even though the plane is only over land and not in the canyon itself, this
still represents a 250 foot difference (i.e. lower than usual).

3. How do I tell if I'm under a cloud?

To determine whether or not you are under a cloud, you should turn and look to your
right at what you normally see as you approach a airport (e.g.. another aircraft,
fence). If you see the ground, airport or other objects that you would normally see
during an approach, then you know that you are not under a cloud.

4. What are some common cloud configurations?

There are various cloud configurations that pilots should be aware of. Some types include:

5. How do I avoid ice?

It's important for pilots to be able to recognize icing conditions and flight levels where icing conditions exist. In the U.S., icing conditions exist between 9K and 14K (18K in Alaska). Air traffic controllers will always specify these flight levels for pilots.

When aircraft approach an airport, air traffic controllers may instruct them to "descend at pilot's discretion." This means that the pilot has the authority from ATC to descend below the cloud cover at any time. Air traffic controller will always state the minimum altitude when issuing instructions to descend (e.g.. "Descend and call 100", or "Descend and maintain 3,000").

Pilots should never exceed a cloud base of 600 feet/200 feet below a cloud base regardless of weather conditions. In icing conditions, icing can still occur if your aircraft is flying above the freezing level, but below a cloud base of 600 feet/200'.

6. What are downdrafts?

Downdrafts occur when a cloud is capable of sucking dry the tops of tall smoke stacks or power lines. When a pilot encounters clusters of these towers, they must be careful as to avoid flying below the top of the towers. The area immediately around the tower can have ice (as well as other hazardous conditions). To avoid this area, the pilot should be aware that they are flying below the top of some towers and change altitude.

Another type of downdraft occurs during high moisture days when pilots fly through nearby cirrus clouds formed by cumulus clouds (which can look like mist) that produce down drafts and turbulence.

7. How amount of time do I have to react?

This question is often not as obvious as it may seem. It depends on what the situation is and how far away you are from the other aircraft.

For example, if a pilot is told to "descend and call 1,000 feet," they need to descend immediately without looking at their altimeter. If a pilot is instructed to "descend and maintain 2,000," then they should ensure that they are 1,000 feet below the target altitude before calling out their speed. The time that pilots have available for any action depends on how much time it will take for them to call out their actions (i.e. "Descending... level... report... check").

8. What altitude do I need to keep?

Often pilots will be told by an air traffic controller that it is "controlled" below a particular level (i.e. "flaps 25, vector for runway 4L, controlled to 2,500 feet"). In these cases, the pilot should not descend below the assigned altitude unless instructed otherwise by air traffic control or unless the situation changes (i.e.. thunderstorms approaching).

Another common instruction can be: "Descend and maintain 3K." In this case, the pilot should not descend below 3K until receiving further instructions from ATC or if other conditions change.

9. What is obstacle clearance?

Obstacle clearance can be defined as the distance from an aircraft that is set clear of any object ahead. Air traffic controllers will specify the exact time and altitude that a pilot must maintain to avoid being hit by other aircraft.

Air traffic controllers will specify obstacles by distances (e.g.. "this traffic is at 1K... keep your heading 090 until you are cleared"). The type of obstacle depends on wind conditions and whether or not the power lines are grounded or suspended (usually for security reasons).

Pilots should remember that ATC does not always have to provide this information on their radio transmissions (e.g.. "Aircraft at 6K... descending and maintaining 4K").

10. An airplane that is claimed to be intrinsically stable will

A. be difficult to stall

B. require less effort to control

C. not spin

An inherently stable airplane will tend to return to its original flight condition if it's disturbed by forces such as the turbulent air. So what that equates to is that a stable airplane will be easier to fly and require less effort to control, which is B.

11. What is the most common cause of accidents? Why?

Lack of Preflight Planning, Poor Preflight Planning, Excuses for not planning (e.g. "I only need to carry one quick reference book with me"), or a combination of the above.

12. What is the proper method to establish weather conditions at airports?

In order to avoid confusion over weather reports and forecasts, it is essential that pilots fly under instrument meteorological conditions. This is accomplished by establishing an accurate location and altitude (ICAO or IFR altitude or pressure altitude). There are several accepted methods for providing this information: 1) Both ICAO and IFR pressure altitudes must be entered into the aircraft's memory using either a pressure altimeter or a radiosonde. 2) When an altitude is entered, the appropriate standard altimeter setting must be selected. The altimeter should be set to read the pressure altitude and set to zero in accordance with local weather reports. 3) A radiosonde may also be used. 4) In the absence of a radiosonde, pilots must establish an accurate location by using Global Positioning System (GPS). If all three methods are properly used, there is sufficient information in the pilot's memory to establish accurate weather conditions at airports.

13. What is the proper method of issuing a clearance by radio?

A pilot can give clearance with an oral transmission or hand signal. Both transmissions should meet FAA requirements for time interval between transmissions (2 minutes). The oral transmission should be in clear, unambiguous language and in a normal conversational tone. A purpose of the oral transmission is to inform the receiving station that you have commenced your flight, not to give a detailed flight plan or relay information concerning the aircraft being flown.

14. What is meant by "Forming", "Rounding", or a "Trail"?

"Forming" comprises maintaining 1/2 statute mile from an airport boundary (land or sea) in the direction of arrival. All aircraft must be within 3 miles of runways when approaching an airport runway by any route at an altitude lower than 1 mile (600 feet). If another aircraft is "trailing", there has been a violation of the separation rules.

The "trailing" aircraft should be brought back into the maneuvering circle by maneuvering controls (e.g., throttle, pitch pedals, or rudder). If another aircraft continues to trail when ordered to remain in position, the trailing aircraft may climb out of its trail until it is ordered to change position. The trailing aircraft must use a turn-and-slip procedure or be forced to break off its trail. If a turn-and-slip procedure is used, the aircraft must be flown in position by using rudder and throttle controls.

15. What is the standard method of avoiding small aircraft ahead?

Due to the absence of an accurate range rate indicator in most small aircraft, pilots must use a lead and lag technique. The lead and lag technique is accomplished by flying at a safe distance behind the aircraft with an imaginary line connecting both aircraft. This line should be at least 2 seconds lead or 1 second lag behind the other aircraft depending on the type of flight being conducted (e.g., normal straight-line flight).

16. What is VFR cruising altitude?

It is safe to fly at altitudes below 10,000 feet MSL which are higher than the highest obstacle within a 15-mile radius of the aircraft's position. A straight-line distance of 15 miles extends outward from the aircraft's position. Pilots may climb to this altitude when outside these lateral limits and when not climbing over a ridge or mountainous area where obstructions cannot be seen.

17. What is defined as hazardous conditions?

Hazardous conditions occur whenever there is precipitation, fog, thunderstorms, icing, or any other condition that makes flight below 10,000 feet unsafe.

18. What are the provisions of a VFR flight plan?

When filing a VFR flight plan, pilots should include airport of departure, intended destination, alternate airport (if applicable), cruising altitude, route of flight and estimated time en route. Pilots should receive an early weather briefing that includes altitude advisories and other necessary information. No IFR clearance is required to depart on a VFR flight plan.

19. What information must be included in a pilot's operating permit?

Applying for an operating permit from the FAA must be done by FAA approved application form 7711-1. This application must include the pilot's name, address and mailing address (if different), the aircraft's identification number and registration, the type of operation to be conducted, as well as a brief description of flight school operations. The information contained in this form has been provided by the Department of Transportation (DOT) and is considered official information. Pilots may e-file for permits using an FAA approved form or obtain a copy from any FAA Flight Standards District Office.

20. What are the principles of straight-line instrument flying?

The cardinal principle involved in straight-line instrument flying is to keep all terrain features on one side of a flight path during each leg of a flight. This is accomplished by using VORs, TACANs and NDBs.

Part 4

1. Describe the difference between the VOR and TACAN locators?

The TACAN provides azimuth, distance and radial to/from a station. The VOR provides azimuth and distance from a station as well as an indication of magnetic track. Those kinds of differences ought to be kept in mind when operating in areas with both facilities available for navigation.

2. What is winds hear? Winds hear is a condition of rapidly changing air velocity that can exist along a narrow frontal zone or within any layer of the atmosphere. The aircraft may lose control and crash during this condition.

3. How do you determine whether or not you are in winds hear? The three basic winds hear indicators are a piper tone, abrupt change of aircraft performance, and the tendency to yaw or roll the aircraft to one side. These indications occur when airspeed drops below normal without a means of leveling out the airplane quickly. If a piper tone is heard, it indicates an almost immediate drop in airspeed accompanied by a steep bank and loss of control. If the pilot maintains control of the aircraft by applying elevator stick force while turning according to direction (e.g., yawing) indicated on the altimeter, flight into terrain should be avoided.

4. How do you avoid winds hear? The basic procedure in avoiding winds hear is to climb while turning according to direction indicated by the flight instruments, maintain a safe vertical distance between the airplane and the terrain, and proceed at normal cruise speed.

5. What are the principles of rivet flying? When maneuvering at low altitudes during instrument conditions (below 7,000 feet MSL), pilots must acquire an accurate fix on a station before lower altitude maneuvering is then permitted. If it will be necessary to commence low altitude flight, it should be coupled with a visual check of weather conditions as well as terrain in order to determine if conditions are favorable for a departure.

6. What is the ideal altitude to maintain while flying in instrument conditions? The ideal altitude to maintain while flying in instrument conditions is at least 1,000 feet AGL. This allows pilots to maneuver with greater accuracy thereby reducing the chances of a collision with terrain.

7. What are some of the disadvantages of low level flight? Some of these disadvantages include: restricted visibility, terrain and obstacles which may obstruct flight paths, reduced wind velocity information, limited ceiling and visibility due to distance from station, and limited radar coverage caused by range gate limitations. The use of minimum safe altitude can reduce these disadvantages and increase safety when weather conditions require VFR operations below 10,000 feet MSL.

8. When flying low level, what must be considered? Pilots must consider obstacles and terrain with different obstacles located at varying distances. Pilots should also consider the loss of altitude that is required to clear each obstacle. These objects can vary in size and shape (e.g., trees).

9. What is the lowest altitude that may be flown during VFR operations? The lowest altitude allowed when VFR conditions exist is 500 feet AGL with a clearance from air traffic control. If an airport permits lower approaches or landings, the absolute minimum VFR altitude must not be less than 300 feet AGL.

10. What is the transponder system? The transponder is a device that receives and electronically processes signals from an aircraft's Mode C or Mode S transponder. The aircraft transmits various data including altitude and direction. The radar altimeter uses this data to determine the exact height of an aircraft, thereby providing terrain clearance information.

11. What is an auto-tune function? An auto-tune function allows the pilot to enable or disable the automatic tuning of a transponder by depressing a switch mounted on the control stick during cruise flight within controlled airspace.

12. What are the benefits of an auto-tune function? The main benefit is an increased level of safety because a pilot is not required to manually tune a transponder every time he or she flies. It also eliminates the possibility of inadvertently not using a transponder.

13. What is a Mode C transponder? A Mode C transponder is used by civilian aircraft for devices that are isolated from ground stations and have no need for link with the radar network. They are intended to give minimum protection, but provide aircraft identification information derived from return echoes to ground stations in order to allow them to identify the aircraft flight and location (altitude and direction, if applicable).

14. What is Mode S? Mode S transponders are similar to Mode C transponders, but are used by civilian aircraft for communication with air traffic control units. They normally give priority to ground station communications and automatically provide the aircraft's altitude and heading information as an aid to collision avoidance, especially during night approaches or in poor visibility conditions. There is normally an audible tone associated with the Mode S transponder which will be heard by ground controllers who use this information to provide them guidance when providing radar services.

15. What are the circumstances under which an error code is displayed on the cockpit's primary flight display? The flying/landing light illuminates only during straight-in operations. A landing approach with an auto land function activated (A/L mode) will illuminate a landing button. If the pilot presses the land button, his or her airplane will be joined by all other airplanes on the same altitude band, and all airplane systems will be activated.

16. What is a NAVAIDS function? NAVAIDS allows a pilot to enter alternate airports in case he or she cannot find their ILS runway or if they are unable to locate their airway, in order to proceed to a programmed alternate airport. NAVAIDS also gives the pilot an alternate airport to use as a diversion in case of weather or other safety concerns.

17. Which way should you look when flying at night so that you can see your wingtip lights? Clear of obstructions and stopped aircraft.

18. What is the last check item before a flight? Equipment (all systems are checked and work properly).

19. When flying in IMC, what is the safe approach speed for a go-around? Vapp + 25 knots indicated airspeed.

20. Who are the 2 main pilots in a flight crew? Pilot Flying and Pilot Monitoring.

21. What instrument is used to determine magnetic variation? The compass card (itis the apparent change of angle between magnetic north and grid north).

Part 5

1. What mode can be used to fly an instrument approach with vertical guidance (either ILS or MLS)? VNAV mode - Vertical Navigation. It is also used to follow vertical guidance of an FMS route (ie: SID).

2. What information will be found on the approach plate?

a) Desired altitude,

b) Minimum altitude,

c) Missed approach instructions if the runway is not in sight,

d) Runway visual range (RVR),

e) Chart numbers for both ends of the runway,

f) Instructions for making a visual approach or circling approach.

3. How does NEXRAD help you as a pilot? It gives you weather radar images which can be used to determine weather conditions of a particular area (approach or departure paths). It also shows where severe weather (thunderstorms, hail, etc.) is located. Additionally it can show turbulence around an area.

4. What is ILS runway designation? The last 3 digits are the mobile airfield identifier, normally something like 33 or 50.

5. Why is it important to use the same runway for landing and for takeoff? For different reasons, both have their hazards. The closer you can get to your final approach waypoint, the less time you will have for maneuvering around a construction zone or an obstacle at or near touchdown height.

6. How many runways does an airport have? 3-4 depending on its size, purpose and type of operation (commercial or private). It can also have an approach (captain) runway as a secondary runway that allows night operations/ landing approaches

7. What happens if the FMS glideslope is set to zero degrees? The airplane automatically follows the glideslope leading to a high rate of descent and if the runway is far enough ahead, you may land into the ground.

8. If a simulated approach plate is shown on approach, what must I do? Use NDB or LNAV to match with your course; monitor the indicated track and runway visual range (RVR)

9. What instrument is used to determine magnetic variation? The compass card (it is the apparent change of angle between magnetic north and grid north).

10. What is an alternate airport? An alternate airport can be used as a diversion in case of weather or other safety concerns.

11. What is the last check item before a flight? Equipment (all systems are checked and work properly)

12. If a simulated approach plate is shown on approach, what must I do? Use NDB or LNAV to match with your course; monitor the indicated track and runway visual range (RVR)

13. What instrument is used to determine magnetic variation? The compass card (it is the apparent change of angle between magnetic north and grid north).

14. How does NEXRAD help you as a pilot? It gives you weather radar images which can be used to determine weather conditions of a particular area (approach or departure paths). It also shows where severe weather (thunderstorms, hail, etc.) is located. Additionally it can show turbulence around an area.

15. What is the last check item before a flight? Equipment (all systems are checked and work properly).

16. What does A-THR stand for? Automatic Thrust Reduction.

17. To what airway system waypoint can you select on the departure procedure page of the FMC to make a turn from a direct course to the airway? The waypoint directly ahead of your track on that particular airway, if there is one in front of you. If there is none, select waypoint 0.

18. What does ATC normally do if it sees a plane on final for an instrument approach that is not holding its assigned extended centerline? If we are in a radar position and see you have not yet made your procedure turn, ATC will ask you to hold short of the runway based on your altitude and location relative to our own radar position. If you are near the FAF, ATC will normally ask you to extend your pattern as a result of your extended final.

19. What kind of weather should a pilot avoid when flying?

- Thunderstorms (if possible).

- Turbulence (if possible)

20. If the aircraft ahead is making a climbing turn, what should you do? If I am behind an aircraft doing a climbing turn on final and continue following at the same rate of descent and airspeed as before, I will increase my rate of descent and speed in relation to his.

Part 6

1. What instrument is used to determine magnetic variation? The compass card (itis the apparent change of angle between magnetic north and grid north).

2. What are the 2 most important flight instruments to look at when flying in IMC? The artificial horizon and the altimeter.

3. What is an alternate airport? An alternate airport can be used as a diversion in case of weather or other safety concerns.

4. What are the 2 most important flight instruments to look at when flying in IMC? The artificial horizon and the altimeter.

5. What is an example of an important control of airspace? The "look-down" or "look-out" provisions of FAR 91.117, which are found in part 99 of the FAR.

6. What is the most useful instrument that you should know how to read? The artificial horizon.

7. What are the 2 most important flight instruments to look at when flying in IMC? The artificial horizon and the altimeter.

8. How does a pilot obtain flight following? Contact the local air traffic control (ATC) center for the airport and request flight following.

9. What is an example of equipment that includes both navigation and communication functions? GPS navigation systems.

10. Which is NOT correct regarding the frequency of ADS-B Out Mode 2? It transmits information about aircraft positions, destination, and intent into ATC via Mode 1 transmissions.

11. Which statement about ADS-B is true? It includes a digital collision avoidance system that detects possible dangers near the aircraft.

12. Is there any difference between the airspace used for flight training and that used for commercial purposes? Yes, there is a 10-mile (16 km) separation between the air traffic control (ATC) service area and an aerodrome where your flight training was **conducted.**

13. What are 3 different types of navigation systems used for flight? VOR, GPS and NDB

14. How much degrees do you need to turn to go from a VOR to the reciprocal VOR? 360/2 = 180 (180 degrees of turn)

15. How much degrees do you need to turn to go from a VOR to the reciprocal VOR? 360/2 = 180 (180 degrees of turn)

16. How many degrees do you need to turn to go from a NDB to the reciprocal NDB? 360 - 120 = 240 (240 degrees of turn)

17. How many degrees do you need to turn when flying from one navigation system beacon at 5,000 ft and another navigation system beacon at 7,000 ft altitudes? 120

18. What is the maximum angle of bank for a glider?

The maximum angle degree of bank for a glider is 45 degrees.

19. What are the 2 most important flight instruments to look at when flying in IMC? The artificial horizon and the altimeter.

20. What is the difference between a flight plan and a clearance? They are both FAA-approved flight instructions that give you specific instructions for your flight but refer to different things like airports, altitudes and equipment used during the flight.

Part 7

1. **What is the FAA's current funding?** $18 billion per year, with about $4 billion coming from user fee revenues such as those paid by pilots and airlines.

2. **Which is not one of the FAA's nine strategic goals?** To establish world-class aviation safety.

3. **What is NOT a benefit of flight training at smaller airports?** Close proximity to major airports where you fly on cross-country trips; no delays due to large numbers of aircraft arriving and departing; ability to get additional training and experience in low-altitude flying; some airports have control towers for radio contact with ATC.

4. **Which statement about FAA rules is correct?** For example, FAR 91.175 prohibits pilots from operating airplanes not having a closed cockpit.

5. **You need to land the airplane after it is hit by lightning. What should you do?** Activate the emergency landing gear and make your best attempt to find strong air currents that will cause your airplane to glide onto the ground without damage.

6. How can you improve fuel conservation and reduce noise pollution? Minimize unnecessary cruising time between fuel stops; use alternate airports as much as possible; fly faster; choose airport locations that allow easy access to all runways; fly through Class B airspace when possible or when ATC requires this action.

7. **Why is weather a consideration when planning for an upcoming trip?** Weather is one of the most important factors in arriving at a destination.

8. **Which band of radio frequencies has the least interference?** The VHF, or Very High Frequency band (144–148 megahertz, or MHz)

9. **How many airlines are now operating in the United States?** There are 730 commercial passenger airlines operating in the United States as of December 31, 2012; that's up from 922 as of December 31, 2010.

10. **How many of the top airlines operate from Dallas-Fort Worth International Airport?** The No. 1 airline from Dallas-Fort Worth (DFW) is American Airlines, with 70 routes, 2.6 million passengers and 18 new airplanes.

11. **What is a primary benefit of flying?** Having a job where you can fly for a living; feeling like you are part of some special group; meeting new people; exercising your intellect and creativity through the design of machines that humans use to travel in the sky; having money saved over the course of your career to spend on additional activities.

12. **Approximately how many flight schools are there in the United States?** About 150,000 student pilots receive training each year at more than 6,000 flight schools and community colleges across the country, with about 13 percent of those students receiving financial aid or scholarships to pay for their training.

13. **Which action helps the pilot avoid wasting fuel during cruise flight?** Staying well within the maximum range of the aircraft; climbing to higher altitude; flying faster at all times; reducing drag by minimizing flaps and other surface areas that can catch wind.

14. **Which is NOT a benefit of NOTIFYONLY?** It helps the pilot identify any updated information that may have been received in the flight plan but not actually "notified" to the pilot.

15. **If an airplane is leaking fuel and you don't know where it is coming from, what should you do?** Stop all forward movements and shut off all fuel pumps until you have located the source of the leak; listen for any popping noises, look for smoke or fire, and visually inspect all parts of the plane.

16. **When checking the weather using a computer, what is the best way to begin?** Click on the map tab and follow the instructions on how to draw an area of interest. Then click on the "fire weather" link for more details about that area.

17. **Which statement about training and flight schools is correct?** The FAA does not conduct audits of flight schools.

18. **How often must you log flight time?** Once every 6 months, but this can vary depending on the number of hours flown per month, combined with the type of aircraft flown and whether or not there have been any changes in the pilot's schedule.

19. **What is the way to permanently remove temporary flight restrictions?** After 30 days, look for a "remove" link in the weather recurrence section of your last ATIS.

20. **Which of the following is one element of VFR weather minimums?**

Answers. Altimeter setting -1,000 feet QNH or 1,000 feet above field elevation if higher than 6,000 feet MSL. (QNE) (or landing field elevation). Pilot –instruments, Pilot –visual, Pilot -radio.

PRACTICE TESTS

1. An amateur pilot who is acting as pilot in command must have in his or her possession while aboard the aircraft

    A. A current logbook endorsement to show that a flight review has been satisfactorily accomplished.

    B. The current and appropriate pilot and medical certificates.

    C. The pilot logbook to show recent experience requirements to serve as pilot in command have been met.

Answer B—Subject Matter Knowledge Code: A29.

2. One of the major functions of flaps during approach and landing is to

    A. Decrease the angle of descent without increasingly the airspeed.

    B. Permit a touch down at a higher indicated airspeed.

    C. Increase the angle of descent without increasingly the airspeed.

Answer C—Subject Matter Knowledge Code: H305.

3. .One of the major functions of flaps during approach and landing is to

    A. Decrease the angle of descent without increasingly the airspeed.

    B. Permit a touch down at a higher indicated airspeed.

    C. Increase the angle of descent without increasingly the airspeed.

Answer C— Subject Matter Knowledge Code: "I21".

4. When telephoning a meteorological briefing facility for pre-flight weather information, pilots shall

    A. Identify themselves as pilots.

    B. Tell the number of hours they have flown within the preceding 90 days.

    C. State the number of occupants on board and the color of the aircraft.

Answer A—Subject Matter Knowledge Code: H320.

5. What action can a pilot take to aid in cooling an engine that is overheating during a climb?

    A. Reduce rate of climb and increase airspeed.

    B. Reduce climb speed and increase RPM.

    C. Increase climb speed and increase RPM.

Answer A—Subject Matter Knowledge Code: H307.

6. What action should the pilot take if engine failure occurs at altitude?

    A. Open the throttle as the collective pitch is raised.

    B. Reduce cyclic back stick pressure during turns.

    C. Lower the collective pitch control, as necessary, to maintain rotor RPM.

Answer C—Subject Matter Knowledge Code: H80.

7. What exception, if any, permits a recreational pilot to act as pilot in command of an aircraft carrying a passenger for hire?

    A. If the passenger pays no other than the operating expenses.

    B. If a donation is being made to a charitable organization for the flight.

    C. There is no exception.

Answer C—Subject Matter Knowledge Code: A29.

8. The lift differential that exists between the advancing main rotor blade and the retreating main rotor blade is known as

    A. Transverse flow effect.

    B. Dissymmetry of lift.

    C. Hunting tendency.

Answer B—Subject Matter Knowledge Code: H71.

9. The amount of water vapor which air can hold depends on the

    A. Dewpond.

    B. Air temperature.

    C. Stability of the air.

Answer B—Subject Matter Knowledge Code: I24.

10. When calling a weather briefing facility for preflight weather information, pilots should state the

    A. Full name & address of the pilot in command.

B. Intended route, destination, and type of aircraft.

C. Radio frequencies to be used.

Answer B—Subject Matter Knowledge Code: H320.

11. A recreational pilot may fly as single occupant of an aircraft at nights while under the general supervision of a flight instructor provided the flight or surface visibility is at least

A. 3 miles.

B. 4 miles.

C. 5 miles.

Answer C—Subject Matter Knowledge Code: A29.

12. What precaution should be taken while taxiing a gyroplane?

A. The cyclic stick should be held in the neutral position at all times.

B. Avoid abrupt control movements when blades are turning.
   The cyclic stick should be held slightly aft of neutral at all times.

Answer B—Subject Matter Knowledge Code: H702.

13. What are characteristics of unstable air?

A. Turbulence and good surface visibility.

B. Turbulence and poor surface visibility.

C. Nimbostratus clouds and good surface visibility.

Answer A—Subject Matter Knowledge Code: I25.

14. When calling a weather briefing facility for preflight weather information, pilots should state

A. The full name and address of the formation commander.

B. That they possess a current pilot certificate.

C. Whether they intend to fly VFR only.

Answer C—Subject Matter Knowledge Code: H320.

15. A below glide slope indication from a tri-color VASI is a

A. Red light signal.

B. Pink light signal.

C. Green light signal.

Answer A—Subject Matter Knowledge Code: J03.

16.In add, to other pre-flight actions for a VFR flight away from the vicinity of the airport of departure, the rules specifically require the pilot in command to
  A. Review traffic control light signal procedures.
  B. Check the accuracy of the navigation equipment & the emergency locator transmitter (ELT).
  C. Establish runway lengths at the destination airports & the aircraft's takeoff & landing distance data.

Answer C—Subject Matter Knowledge Code: B07.

17. While on cruise at 9,500 feet MSL, the fuel/air blend is properly set. What if you descend to 4,500 feet MSL without re-adjusting the mixture?
  A. The fuel/air blend may become exceedingly lean.
  B. There will be as much fuel in the cylinders as needed for normal combustion, the extra fuels will absorb the heat & cool the engine.
  C. The over-rich mixture will build higher temperatures in the cylinder head & may cause detonation.

Answer A—Subject Matter Knowledge Code: H307.

18. What is the purpose of a flight review?

A. To renew a pilot certificate.

B. To exercise the privileges of a pilot certificate.

C. To determine that the pilot is familiar with essential aircraft systems.

D. To determine that the pilot is proficient in emergency procedures and operations.

Answer: C

19. When should a pilot-in-command (PIC) refuse an assignment of a specific altitude by ATC?

A. When it is not safe for the aircraft to climb or descend at that specific altitude due to nearby conflicting air traffic or unusual pilot workload.

B. When the assigned altitude would subject the aircraft to a severe wake turbulence encounter.

C. When there are no weather reports or forecasts indicating possible turbulence between the present position and any point along the course being flown.

D. When ATC has requested a specific altitude for aircraft operations, but does not furnish the information necessary to make that altitude safely.

Answer: A

20. Which of the following is true about the private pilot certificate?

A. Privileges are limited to private operations only and are specifically denied for commercial operations.

B. Privileges are limited to private operations and include commercial operations in single-engine land airplanes with restrictions as to type and number of passengers, crewmembers, cargo, and type or class of aircraft.

C. Privileges are limited to private operations and include commercial operations in single-engine land airplanes with only a maximum of five occupants, including the pilot.

D. Privileges are limited to private operations and include commercial operations in single-engine land airplanes with a maximum of six occupants, including the pilot.

Answer: D

21. Which two methods can be used vertically to find the height above ground level from which to make adjustments for altitude reference?

A. From a base elevation obtained from a reliable source

B. From an aeronautical chart

C. From the aeronautical information publication (AIP)

D .From the altimeter setting on instruments

E. From the estimated height above ground level that can be obtained from a visual reference

Answer: A

22. What information must be included in a letter of authorization? (More than 1 is correct)

A. Name of the pilot being authorized.

B. Type and model of aircraft involved.

C. Purpose and duration of flight with dates and times involved.

D. Type, quantity and any special handling requirements for freight or passengers in addition to the pilot.

Answer: A, C

23. Which statement concerning the VOR is true?

A. The letter in the center of the VOR indicates its function.

B. The calibration of a VOR is checked by rotating an antenna through 360 degrees.

C. The dots that radiate from the VOR indicate wind velocity and direction.

D. A VOR can be calibrated by rotating an antenna through 360 degrees or by using charts provided with the VOR equipment.

Answer is B

24. Which statement concerning weight-and-balance forms is true? (More than 1 is correct)

A. They are designed for use as permanent records of each flight and remain with the pilot's logbook file throughout his or her career as a pilot.

B. They must be maintained on board the aircraft and in a readily accessible place for any official who may have a reason to inspect them.

C. They are designed for use after each flight and must be destroyed at the end of the Month or at the completion of every 100 Hours.

D. They are designed for use after each flight, but only if that flight involves an essential load.

Answer: B & C

25. What is NOT a primary responsibility of the pilot? (More than 1 is correct)

A. Reporting to an FAA Flight Service Station with weather information during preflight planning and filing an IFR flight plan using that information.

B. Entering the weather observations and special remarks in the logbook.

C. Converting the altimeter setting to appropriate indicated airport elevation.

D. Following all local, state and federal aviation rules, regulations and statutes.

Answer: A & D

26. Which part of a visual flight rules (VFR) flight plan is used for arrivals in Class B airspace? (More than 1 is correct)

A. The filed flight plan.

B. The non-controlled airport information (NAI) included on the filed flight plan.

C. The controlled facility information (CFIT) furnished by ATC to which the aircraft is assigned a specific frequency and that must be filed by air traffic control (ATC).

D. The assigned transponder code, if one is assigned to the aircraft.

E. Contact information, such as telephone numbers, that can be used to contact ATC.

Answer: C & E

27. If you fly from a low pressure zone to a high pressure zone without the altimeter setting being adjusted, the altimeter will show

    A.   The actual altitude above sea level.

    B.   Higher than the actual altitude at sea level.

    C.   Lower than the actual altitude at sea level.

Answer C—Subject Matter Knowledge Code: I22.

28. How is the engine operation controlled on an engine with a constant speed propeller?

    A.   The throttle controls the power output as noted on the manifold gauge and the propeller controls adjust the engine speed.

    B.   The throttle controls the power out put as recorded on the manifold gauge & the propeller controller adjusts a uniform blade angle.

    C.   The throttle controls engine RPM as registered on the tachometer & the mixture control regulates the power output.

Answer A—Subject Matter Knowledge Code: H308.

29. One weather phenomenon which will always occur when flying across a front is a change in the

    A. Wind direction.

    B. Type of precipitation.

    C. Stability of the air mass.

Answer A—Subject Matter Knowledge Code: I27.

30. Which initial action should a pilot take prior to entering Class C airspace?

    A. Contact approach control on the appropriate frequency.

    B. Contact the tower & request permission to enter.

    C. Contact the FSS for traffic advisories.

Answer A—Subject Matter Knowledge Code: J11

FEDERAL AVIATION REGULATIONS (FAR) REFERENCES

Federal Aviation Regulations (FARs) cover the civil aviation system in the United States, and are published by the Federal Aviation Administration. FAA website provides a lot of free information on FARs, including links to Part 1 to Part 25 of FARs. The FARs also govern air traffic control and airspace protection, as well as aircraft certification standards.

Federal Aviation Regulations (FAR) references are regulations of the United States Department of Transportation that adopt international aviation standards and are applicable to civil aviation in the United States. They are published in title 14 of the Code of Federal Regulations. There are many references in these documents, which have been revised over eight times since 1948, with a current revision last updated on April 11, 2017. They are divided into Parts, with each part containing several sections, containing multiple paragraphs.

The Code of Federal Regulations (CFR) is updated annually on January 1, while the FAR's are updated four times each year with the publication date and effective date listed by section. The regulations in 14 CFR have been in effect since June 17, 1940 and have been amended at least 3,264 times as of May 6, 2017.

Federal Aviation Regulations is a set of rules and procedures which an airline must abide by if it wants to carry passengers in one of its aircrafts. These regulations are maintained by the United States Department of Transportation, or DOT. The FAR references are policies and guidelines that help demonstrate what is expected from airlines when it comes to carrying passengers.

The goals of these regulations is to make sure that passengers are safe and are not at risk of death or injury during an airline flight. When flying, airlines are required to obey these regulations. These regulations include things such as when a pilot must use the intercom system and when they must break their radio silence on certain occasions.

On a general basis, FAR references contain two main parts: Part 91, which deals with rules concerning flights in US airspace, and Part 135, which deals with rules concerning international flights. The FAR contains all rules about passenger safety and requires that airlines do everything possible to adhere to these regulations.

In the US, there is a departmental organization known as the Federal Aviation Administration. This is the organization that maintains and develops FAR. The FAA can give out civil penalty fines to anyone who does not follow these regulations and/or have their operations certificate revoked.

Airworthiness directives signed by FAA Administrator that must be followed in order to have airworthiness approval of fleet or a type of aircraft. These directives may contain maintenance, operation, design, quality assurance, safety, or security changes and must be met within specified limits set forth by the directive and in accordance with the FAR. The FAA issues these directives to protect public health and safety on the basis of information obtained from surveillance reports filed by civil aviation organizations around the world that track aircraft airframes damaged during certain abnormal conditions such as sudden decompression events (e.g., cracks during pressurization). The FAA also issues a variety of letters and other summaries that are not covered as directives; these are referred to as advisory circulars (AC). For example, Advisory Circular 99-4-2, titled "Propellers on Large Domestic Airplanes," advises operators of aircraft with propellers of more than 15 inches (38 cm) in diameter to use modified propeller tips.

Aircraft is certified only after proper inspection and approval by an approved organization that has performed the required tests on the aircraft and determined it to be qualified. FAA inspectors perform initial inspections and provide certification inspections on each model year throughout the production cycle. The FAA has no authority to order aircraft or airframe manufacturers to conduct any inspection or test for certification. However, FAA certification inspections are conducted by the FAA and are designed to ensure that products of airworthiness regulations are manufactured according to accepted commercial practices and installed in accordance with the type certificate. The FAA carries out these activities in cooperation with other government agencies: other federal, state, county and municipal governments; universities; consultants; aviation industry organizations; and commercial and military pilots from around the world.

FAA REGULATION REQUIRES FOR GA AIRCRAFT

F AA regulation requires all GA aircraft flying in controlled airspace to be equipped with a two-way radio and a transponder. Aircraft without these components may fly in uncontrolled airspace, but when flying through controlled space they will be required to wire the area frequency on board and monitor it continually for traffic information. The average cost of a two-way radio is $550 and an ADS-B position source $1500 - $2000. Answer for DPE

The GA aircraft market is extremely competitive and growing as a result of the increased number of GA aircraft and the rising interest in general aviation. The FAA has reported that more than 540,000 GA aircraft were registered from 2005 to 2013 and that number continues to increase by about 10,000 per year. In recent years, new products have been introduced into the market designed for more efficient, safer flying.

For GA aircraft owners:

There is a demand for all types of GA planes; however, larger planes are seen as a good investment because they often cost less than smaller planes. Experienced pilots are interested in aircraft that can be flown cross-country without having to stop and refuel. Fractional ownership companies have increased in popularity. They offer pilots a chance to own a share of an aircraft without the burden of maintaining and flying the plane. Share owners can also share the costs of renting and maintenance with other owners, which often lowers the individual cost of flying.

For GA aircraft manufacturers:

New models are entering the market every year, which increases competition for manufacturers trying to capture this growing market. Manufacturers must decide between producing an updated version of an existing model or start from scratch with a new model entirely.

For GA aircraft renters:

Renters are looking for planes that can be used for longer travel and offer a more comfortable flying experience. Convenience is vital to renters, so they prefer aircraft that can be delivered and picked up from the airport. This reduces the time between making a reservation and actually getting into the air by days or weeks. This has led to somewhat of a "disposable" mentality among owners; however, it still increases the demand for GA aircraft.

For GA aircraft mechanics:

Aircraft mechanics are in high demand because of the increasing number of aircraft in the fleet and the need for maintenance on each individual plane. As a result, many colleges have introduced specialized courses focused on aircraft maintenance.

Maintenance tasks have changed from an eight-hour day with an eight-hour weekend to a twelve-hour day with an eight-hour weekend, according to a University of Southern Florida study. With this shift in utility, equipment purchases have gone digital, which means that they can be programmed and easy to operate. This will allow mechanics to spend less time learning the equipment and more time keeping up with a growing fleet. For owners and manufacturers, an increasing focus on GA aircraft is on safety. A report from the Air Safety Institute indicated that from 2010 to 2011 there was a 9.3% increase in reported accidents involving single-engine planes; however, this decrease may be attributed to the FAA's Early Aviation and General Aviation Accident Prevention (EAGAAPP) program. The program targets "high-risk pilots" as well as aircraft flying over 10,000 ft. AGL or spending more than 16 hours in the air per month, which accounts for around 90% of total GA flight hours per year.

According to the FAA:

"The GA aircraft fleet is aging, and as older planes are retired, the average age of all U.S. registered airplane increases." This percentage of older aircraft has been increasing since 2005 and "the FAA expects that this trend will continue into the future."

In addition to aging aircraft, there is an increase in weight restrictions on GA aircraft. The weight limitations on GA aircraft are based on both maximum takeoff rating (MTR) parameters set by the manufacturers as well as aerodynamic characteristics. Due to the limitations of both factors, GA aircraft must fly slower; therefore, they are a safer option than larger jets. These weight restrictions place a greater emphasis on safety in order to maintain an overall safe flying environment. The FAA has stated that it is "committed to ensuring that the safe operation of GA aircraft will continue for the foreseeable future."

DIFFERENCES BETWEEN GROUND SCHOOLS

If you are trying to expand your aviation industry knowledge, you might be wondering which ground schools are best. Don't fret about having to wade through hours of internet research or scouring through what can sometimes feel like a never-ending list of options. After reading it, you'll have a much better idea about what you should be looking for in an aviation program and how to evaluate potential organizations. We also cover internship opportunities for those who are interested in getting their feet wet with real-world experience before graduation. This book compares the differences between various professional aviation schools. These include:

Flight Schools – Gain practical experience from the start with a flight school. Flight programs have become increasingly popular in recent years, and for good reason. A flight school can provide you with invaluable experience at an affordable price. While most schools are centered on training pilots how to fly, some also offer courses relating to maintenance and other related fields.

Ground Schools – For aspiring pilots with a desktop background, you might introduce yourself with a ground school. While less hands-on than flight schools, ground schools can provide valuable theoretical knowledge that'll allow you learn to read and understand the information that's necessary to understand how air traffic control works and how the airspace around airports are arranged.

Professional Scoring Organizations – Professional performance organizations, like the Commercial Pilot's Licensing Exam (CPL) and Airframe & Power plant Licensing Exam (A&P), assess your skill level in order to determine your training status in relation to certified pilots.

Professional Pilot Training – A professional training program can offer you a step up from the typical flight or ground school. These programs can provide a more comprehensive approach that's centered on preparing pilots for the real world. Professional pilot training programs are also known to be highly competitive.

Professional Pilot Licensing – Once you've obtained your professional license, you will have the certification necessary to fly commercial flights and large groups of passengers. In order to obtain this license, it's crucial that you possess flight hours under your belt as well as obtain professional scoring through organizations like CPL and A&P. If you've been accepted into a professional pilot training program, then you may be able to bypass these requirements. This is because these schools are designed to prepare students for their professional license once they graduate.

Professional Pilot Employment – If you've obtained a professional pilot license, it's likely that you'll be granted the opportunity of helping to operate flights for some of the most prominent airlines in the industry. Corporate and private planes also offer job opportunities for pilots.

Professional Air Shows – Many airports will host air shows on a regular basis, which are designed to put pilots in control of their own airshows with the goal of entertaining large numbers of people.

Ground schools are a way for you to learn about various disciplines and get licensed in a field without spending years of your life and thousands of dollars to do so. They typically cost less than $5,000, but they have the same rigor as any other school that is out there. The difference between them is that they prepare you to take an entry-level job with little experience in the field. For students who tend to be impatient, this might be their best chance at finally getting what they want from school without spending 10+ years doing it. However, if you're looking for credit hours or degrees that show on your resume or college applications, these schools won't help you much further than earning certificates like "First Aid. The difference between the two is the length and amount of time you are required to spend in classes. A general diploma looks like the one below:

A diploma for this job will earn you a degree in: electrical engineering technology. The school mentions that it is not accredited by any body, but it does have a "programmatic accreditation through ABET". This means that they pay to get evaluated by them, or it could mean that they have similar policies like them. These schools typically offer 16 hours at 1 credit per hour, which would mean that they would require you to be there for one year at 8 hours per day, 5 days a week.

The average college course is approximately 6 weeks. Let's say that you took an online college course in this field. The major difference between these two is the degree earned, and the fact that it is 1 credit versus 16 credits. These degrees are worth more than regular ones because you have spent the same amount of time learning and have the same knowledge as someone who has spent 4 years in school. Most companies would prefer an employee with a degree over one with a diploma, but they are both considered equal.

Make sure to research any school that is looking to hire examinees from them. You don't want to work for a shady school that is only looking for your money. A diploma will always be higher in the job market even though a degree will look better on paper.

USEFUL ADDRESSES OF GROUND AND ONLINE SCHOOLS

Whether you're pursuing an aviation career or simply want to pursue one as a hobby, it's important to ensure that your education is up to date. With the rise in students and advancements in technology, online schools are becoming more popular than ever. So if you're considering changing your career, or simply want to learn a new skill for personal enrichment, these schools offer courses on everything from aviation training and piloting certificates to math tests and other essential topics. For those individuals aspiring towards an education as a pilot, anyone can join ground schools for free at any of these websites. Again, these are free, so you should check them out and see where they fit in your future.

UAV University https://www.uavu.com/

UAV University offers a wide range of skills including full instruction for beginners who do not have any experience with UAV's and want extensive information on how to get started in the field. They offer video trainings, written and video instructions as well as online courses that can be completed at your own pace. They also offer free training through their website that goes over the basics of how to fly a drone. This website is awesome for those individuals who want to get started quickly if they don't have any prior experience with UAVs or pilot controls in general. If you have experience, however, you should look into the premium courses.

Seattle Pacific University https://www.spu.edu/aviation/

This University offers a wide range of aviation specific classes and career information for students interested in becoming a pilot as well as looking to better their skillset with online courses that can be taken through your home computer or mobile device. They offer online training and career preparation in many different areas of aviation, such as chart navigation, flight theory, and course management and administration. The courses they offer are suited towards all skill levels; so if you're just getting started or are an experienced pilot with years of experience on your resume, they can help you develop your skills further.

The University of Nebraska-Lincoln https://www.nebraska.edu/aviation

The University of Nebraska-Lincoln offers both ground training and online courses through their Aviation Institute. They offer flight training in both the fixed wing and rotorcraft areas. None of their courses are free, but varies in pricing depending on the length of time, desired certification or advanced course requirements for your .ocular career path. The institute also offers a $100 application fee that does not need to be paid until your initial enrollment date, which is at least 10 days prior to the program start date; however there are no other fees for admission or enrollment after this point.

Pima Medical Institute http://pimamedicalinstitute.com/

Pima Medical Institute is an all-access pass that has access to over 24,000 videos and over 900 courses available to view anytime. This includes courses on everything from CPR and life safety to a free course on UAV flight operations.

Columbia   Southern   University
https://www.columbiasouthernuniversity.edu/aviation-studies

Columbia Southern University offers a number of free classes on topics such as aviation management and certification, commercial flight education and training and many more. They also offer a number of aviation courses that you can take remotely through your home computer or mobile device. Many of the courses available through their Aviation Studies Major are transferrable to other schools around the country so you can work towards your bachelor's degree completely online with Columbia Southern University.

Western Michigan University http://www.wmich.edu/AV/

Western Michigan University offers online learning in both aviation & aerospace with various types of certifications available to students within the field. Their online programs are all free to enroll in, however various tests and classes may require payment for grading or assessment purposes. For those individuals looking to become a commercial pilot, Western Michigan University offers online training in both instrument ground school and flight training.

Auburn University http://www.auburn.edu/

Auburn University offers aviation courses and training though the Auburn University Aviation Center of Excellence. This is a non-profit center that provides instruction to individuals looking to build their resume and earn professional certifications in aviation management, operations, maintenance and more. Through this center you can learn how to build a resume, apply for jobs and take professional tests; all without leaving the comfort of your home.

University of Arizona https://aviation.arizona.edu/

The University of Arizona offers online courses and courses at various times throughout the week, allowing you to take advantage of their placement assistance services and curriculum that is tailored for aviation professionals who are looking to enter or exit the field. You can also enroll in their Aviation Degree program which includes undergraduate & graduate levels in aviation management and operations as well as an aviation safety program that provides students with all the tools they need to become an aviation professional.

Many opportunities and online pilot schools

Although many universities offer training and courses in aviation, the following are examples of online flight schools or institutions that provide training exclusively online:

Many private pilot applicants pass their knowledge exams using websites designed to aid them with training. "The Complete Private Pilot" by Terry O'Neil, a book originally published in 1984 and now in its seventh edition, is the most reviewed source of private pilot information available on the Internet.

An increasing number of free websites are also available to help potential students explore aviation training and general questions about flight. Some of these sites include interactive simulations to help clarify concepts about flight operations. Online pilot schools are a unique opportunity for individuals to learn to fly planes in a short period of time.

With the fast-paced changes in aviation, and with weather conditions changing at the drop of a hat, there are new requirements that pilots have to keep up with. Online pilot schools can provide hands-on experience that is difficult if not impossible in traditional learning environments.

Below is the list of affordable online pilot schools you may want to consider:

1) International Flight Academy - This school offers hands-on instruction in flying Cessna 172s or Piper Warriors. Students must pass FAA written and practical exams to receive a license. They offer Student Pilot (Private), Instrument Rating, Commercial, and CFI. An intensive Practical Test Preparation Course is available for student pilots preparing for their FAA Practical Examinations. IFA also offers video of each flight lesson in case the student wants to review a lesson they received while they were absent; ideal for individuals schedule that may not permit them to be present every day of class;

2) Learn To Fly Now - This school offers all courses that are necessary to become a pilot except the FAA written exam which is required after the completion of all flight instruction. This school offers a free course called "Captain Your Own Plane." This course provides information regarding aviation, as well as aviation careers;

3) The AOPA Air Safety Foundation - This foundation is affiliated with the American Association of Pilots. They offer three courses: Flight Safety, General Airline Training, and Helicopter Training. They also offer a variety of resources for pilots who are interested in other flight-related topics such as navigation and weather. The courses are all accessible from your home computer;

4) Avion Simulators - This school trains students to fly safely in real world scenarios via virtual reality simulation software. Students learn to fly single-engine, multi-engine and instrument aircraft in an environment similar to real world flying. They offer an extended course which provides more training, and you can be certified as an instrument rated pilot;

5) Aeroseb - This school offers a very detailed course on flying. This course provides operating information on typical single-engine light aircraft and how they are configured. The basic principles of flight are taught through a series of videos that are designed to be easy to understand;

6) Airplane Sim - This school offers training in a simulator from the comfort of your own home. The company offers virtual reality technology that allows you to virtually experience being in the cockpit. They offer their Virtual Reality Flights where they take you on a simulated flight through the cockpit of your own plane. The simulator has a large fish-eye display that gives you an expansive view of the airfield and surrounding areas;

7) AirplaneSim Academy - this school is a subsidiary of AirplaneSim. They offer virtual reality flights also, they are very similar to AirplaneSim but they do not include the full course and only allow you to finish up to being an instrument rated pilot. They also do not allow you to fly multi-engine aircraft;

8) Airplane Sim Tutorial Courses - this program allows you to take a class at home and pay an instructor to give you lessons using the simulator software. This is a great option if you are unable to find an instructor to teach you privately and want someone to guide your learning;

9) Airworks Academy - This school offers trainee pilots who need more training the opportunity to further their education through an in-classroom learning environment. The school trains its students on the proper use of an S-TEC '240' Flight Computer software. Students learn how to use the computer through on-screen training and take a written ground school test. They offer training courses that range from Private, Instrument, Commercial, and CFI. Their training courses are only available at the academy;

10) Aviator Pilot Training - This company allows you to fly planes right in your own community or home. They offer aerobatics, night flying and instrument training courses. This company also offers flight instruction for Pilots with Visual

Disabilities. They also offer Risk Management Training for pilots who are looking to improve their aviation safety record. Their facilities include a simulated instrument panel and a flight instructor to teach you how to fly;

11) **Airforce-Flying** - This company is an online flight school but offers in-classroom training if that is something you are interested in. The courses they offer are the Private Pilot, Instrument Rating, Commercial Pilot, Multi-Engine Rating, Certified Flight Instructor (CFI), & Certified Flight Instructor Instrument (CFII). All courses are FAA approved and provide guidance on how to become a better pilot;

12) **Flying Club Network** - This online school offers flights in many different planes, including planes that you will likely never be able to fly a second time. They offer a very special opportunity to fly in an open cockpit bi-plane with only the sky around you. You get the chance to feel like Jackie Chan in the movie Top Gun where he flies a fighter jet in an air show;

13) **Flight Training Duty Time Calculator**-This is an online calculator for pilots who want to calculate duty times for their flight training. Duty time calculations are important for pilots when they want to fly the same day they have already flown. Duty time is calculated in hours and minutes. The calculator also offers advice for pilots on how to keep their duty times at a minimum;

14) **Aviation Logbook**-This is a website that allows you to log your flight hours and print out any necessary documents such as Certificates of Completion or training records. This site is great because it saves you from having to write your flight hours down on paper and then hand write those numbers onto official documents, which can be very difficult;

15) **Dr. Gizmo** - This website has a ton of great tools that can help any pilot. Some of the tools include a Flight Map that shows your route and flight time, an airport map that helps you plan for arrivals and demurs, a weather balloon Viewer, a course planner tool and an air traffic viewer.

16) **FAA** - This is the go-to website for all things aviation related. It contains information about licenses, planes, pilot testing, regulations etc... It is very helpful if you ever have a question about anything aviation related;

17) **Online Ground School** - This ground school website offers online lessons to help you pass your written tests quickly. The lessons are very thorough and include an unlimited number of questions with answers to help you pass your test. They also offer courses for other written tests;

18) **Airports Near Me** - This is a great website for pilots who want to know details about their local airport. It gives pilots information about their local airports including: runway length, elevation, grass length, helipad type, terrain type and

much more! This is helpful for any pilot who wants to learn about their local area before they fly there;

19) Aviation Weather - This website has detailed information on aviation weather and how it directly affects flying. There are detailed descriptions on everything from the cloud formations to turbulence. This is a great website for pilots who want to learn about the weather before they fly to ensure that they are able to fly safely;

20) Pilot Exam Prep - This is an online exam prep website. It has a ton of different tools and resources available which can help you prepare for the FAA written exams. You will find things such as study outlines, sample questions, practice tests, flash cards and more;

21) Pilot Test Prep - This website has a ton of free resources that can help you prepare for your pilot test. It has sample tests, question answer explanations and practice tests. It is a great website for pilots who are looking to improve their knowledge in preparation for their test;

22) Flight Crew License Guide - This website is a subscription based service that offers course subscriptions and eBooks.

Flight Schools

The alternative to finding an instructor is attending flight school. As mentioned previously, flight schools offer incredible service, arranging both ground and flight training into lectures, providing you with the facilities and equipment to practice as conveniently and regularly as possible and organizing the aircraft, fuel, and maintenance, among others. While flight school costs more than the self-study route, it does streamline the process of getting your FAA PPL.

CONCLUSION

The Private Pilot License FAA Knowledge Check ride is the test to pass in order to obtain a Private Pilot License. It is not for just anyone, however, it is a test that only those who are interested in aviation should take. It has many objectives which include: knowledge of airspace, aerodynamics and flight instruments, as well as complex maneuvers such as stalls, spins and climbs/descents with various weights. These tests are lengthy and can be very challenging so it is important for an individual to prepare themselves properly during their training period for this exam.

An individual should dedicate about 70 hours of flight time before taking the exam which could be taken at any airport within the United States or Canada. After every 10 hours of flight time an individual can take a test as well. If an individual has completed the Private Pilot License FAA Knowledge Checkride exam successfully they will have earned the title of "Private Pilot" and they can fly within all controlled airspace. Preparation and concentration are essential to successfully complete the test. The FAA offers a free online course that can assist with the knowledge exam preparation process so that pilots can be best prepared for their test date.

If you take an online course, be sure to set aside a full day to devote to studying. The problems and questions are extensive, and it's best if the applicant is well rested when tackling the test — both physically and mentally. The time that a pilot spends preparing for the FAA Knowledge Exam is time well spent, though, as it ensures that your future as a pilot will be safe and sound. Your preparation will also lessen your chances of failing the exam by allowing you to steer clear of trouble spots.

We hope that the theory part, the preparation tests and the questions and answers you have found in this manual have helped you to practice and be prepared for your exam.

We sincerely wish you to fulfill your wishes.

SPECIAL BONUS

D ear user, I would appreciate it if you would spend a minute of your time and post a ***short review on AMAZON*** to let other users know about this experience and what you liked most about the book. Also, as of recently**),** I decided to do a giveaway to all our readers. Yes, I want to **give you 3 gifts.**

1. To help you with your study, **the audiobook will be free for you**. It will help you to go over the information by listening to it and imprinting the concepts in your mind. You will surely enjoy the interactive tests: you will have time to reflect and learn dynamically.
2. You will also receive **practical tips** that we hope will help you focus and pass your exam with flying colors.
3. Plus: **300 FLASHCARDS TO USE FOR FREE** IN YOUR ANKI APP (mobile or web) Download the ANKI app to your device and upload the apkg. files we give you as a gift-you can track your progress and conveniently and interactively memorize the most important terms and concepts!

*NOTE: Includes the digital color version for a better visual experience of the images!

Below you will find a **QR CODE** that will give you **direct access** to these bonuses *without having to subscribe to any mailing list or leave your data.* **We hope you enjoy it.**

To communicate with us directly, please write to us at
readers.help.info@gmail.com

A friendly greeting, we wish you the best.

THANK YOU!

Made in the USA
Monee, IL
19 July 2023

39562542R00098